BODY WORK

Reassessing experimental psychology from a critical perspective, Sylvia Blood demonstrates how its research into Body Image can be misused and prone to misuse. Classifying women who experience distress and anxiety with food, eating and body size as suffering 'body image disturbance' or 'body image dissatisfaction', it can reproduce dominant assumptions about language, meaning and subjectivity. Experimental psychology's discourse about body image has recently become more widely influential, becoming popularised through domains such as women's magazines, in which psychological experts provide 'facts' about women's 'body image problems', and offer advice and psychological treatments. With acute cross-disciplinary awareness *Body Work: The Social Construction of Women's Body Image* exposes the assumptions at work in the methods and status of experimental approaches. Penetrating beyond the usual dichotomy between experimental and popular psychology, this book illuminates some of the ways in which women's magazines have embraced experimental psychology's treatment of the issue. Drawing on her experience in clinical psychology, Sylvia Blood highlights the damaging effects of uncritically experimental views of body image. She goes on to elaborate not only an alternative model of discursive construction but also the implications of such a theory for clinical practice.

Merging theory and clinical experience, Sylvia Blood exposes the fallacies about women's bodies that underpin experimental psychology's body image research. She demonstrates the dangerous consequences of these fallacies being accepted as truths in popular texts and in the talk of 'everyday' women.

Sylvia Blood is a Clinical Psychologist who has been in private practice for over fifteen years. She has a particular interest in working with women who experience distress with their bodies and eating.

WOMEN AND PSYCHOLOGY
Series Editor: Jane Ussher
School of Psychology,
University of Western Sydney

This series brings together current theory and research on women and psychology. Drawing on scholarship from a number of different areas of psychology, it bridges the gap between abstract research and the reality of women's lives by integrating theory and practice, research and policy.

Each book addresses a 'cutting edge' issue of research, covering such topics as post-natal depression, eating disorders, theories and methodologies.

The series provides accessible and concise accounts of key issues in the study of women and psychology, and clearly demonstrates the centrality of psychology to debates within women's studies or feminism.

The Series Editor would be pleased to discuss proposals for new books in the series.

BODY WORK

The social construction of women's body image

Sylvia K. Blood

Routledge
Taylor & Francis Group

LONDON AND NEW YORK

First published 2005
by Routledge
27 Church Road, Hove, East Sussex BN3 2FA

Simultaneously published in the USA and Canada
by Routledge
270 Madison Avenue, New York, NY 10016

Routledge is an imprint of the Taylor & Francis Group

© 2005 Psychology Press

Typeset in Times by
Keystroke, Jacaranda Lodge, Wolverhampton
Printed and bound in Great Britain by
MPG Books Ltd, Bodmin, Cornwall

Paperback cover design by
Terry Foley at Anú Design

This publication has been produced with paper manufactured to
strict environmental standards and with pulp
derived from sustainable forests.

British Library Cataloguing in Publication Data
A catalogue record for this book is available from the British Library

Library of Congress Cataloging in Publication Data
Blood, Sylvia K., 1957–
  Body work : the social construction of women's body image / Sylvia K. Blood. – 1st ed.
    p. cm.
  Includes bibliographical references and index.
  ISBN 0–415–27271–8 (hardcover) – ISBN 0–415–27272–6 (pbk.)
  1. Body image in women. I. Title

BF697 .5 .B63B58   2005
306 . 4'613–dc22

27.00   2005000602

ISBN 0–415–27271–8 (hbk)
ISBN 0–415–27272–6 (pbk)

FOR SAM

CONTENTS

CONTENTS

ACKNOWLEDGEMENTS

Margie Wetherell inspired me with her enthusiasm for this project and provided invaluable support. Alison Jones has been a generous teacher and an excellent supervisor. My thanks to Jane Ussher for encouraging me to write this book.

Support from friends and colleagues has been invaluable. Kimberly Farmer, Barbara Grant, Susie Jacka, Sue Jackson, Anne Kennedy and Jennifer Little commented on earlier drafts of this book and sustained me with their faith in this work. Thanks to Aroha Waipara-Panapa and my sister Michelle Gordon for helpful discussions and to Tamsin Hunter for her encouragement. My thanks to Glenn Bradburn for his practical and emotional support. Thanks once again to Todd Brackley for his support and computer assistance.

I extend my gratitude to the women who generously shared their experiences with me.

Permissions

Thanks to ACP publishing for permission to reproduce extracts from their *More* (1992) magazine article on body image (including extracts from Morris, 1992).

Acknowledgement

An earlier version of Chapter 4 was published in *SITES*, 'Radical Perspectives on Culture' (Blood, Spring, 1994).

INTRODUCTION

Anita, a woman in her mid-40s, comes to see me. She is distressed. Crying, she tells me she is fat, that she hates her body and is deeply ashamed about the way she looks. Anita says she is always thinking about food and either restricting what she eats or eating 'everything in sight'. She feels out of control around food. Anita believes that if she could just lose 14 lbs she would feel better about herself. Her body has been a source of distress for her since she was a young woman. She has dieted, without success, since she was 15 and says of her attempts to lose weight, 'I am constantly failing at what is the most important thing in my life'. Later in the session I learn she is facing possible redundancy from her job, her elderly mother is unwell and she is having difficulties with her adolescent son. She is reluctant to talk about these things and appears anxious lest the focus of our talk shifts from her real problem, her body, to these other, lesser issues.

Ten years ago or even five, when women talked about being unhappy with their bodies and eating too much, a discourse of body-reduction through dieting dominated explanations for their difficulties. Women talked about the need to lose weight and to exert greater self-control around food. Failure to lose weight or to maintain weight loss was attributed to their lack of will-power. More recently, experimental psychology's discourse of 'body image problems' has become an increasingly dominant explanation for women's distressing experience of their bodies. Body image discourse supplies a disturbing vocabulary and narrative by which women are understood by others, and understand themselves, as women with a psychological problem of body image dissatisfaction or body image disturbance. These classifications provide answers for the body image experts and become common-sense knowledge about women's painful and distressing experiences of their bodies.

Experimental psychology's theories about body image have become accepted as 'truths', providing scientific explanations for women's concern and distress about their bodies. These 'truths' impact upon women through a process of subjectification. Via popular women's magazines, a discourse of body image problems is woven into the fabric of our everyday experience. The 'truth' about women's body image problems is presented in a persuasive, compelling, plausible manner. Information about body image is presented to women as something all women

1

'have', as something that can be identified and measured according to scientific 'norms' and as something women should know and be concerned about. Women are encouraged to learn about body image, to learn about themselves. Self-scrutiny, confessions and public revelations of women's bodies/subjectivities are actively encouraged in body image articles. The 'findings' of experimental psychology's body image research, reproduced in popular women's magazines, have damaging social implications for women's lives, in particular, for the ways women can experience embodiment.

Within experimental psychology's body image research, objective measurement is often held to be the route to knowledge about women's bodies. The concept of 'body image' is based on fundamental epistemological assumptions about the nature of the mind, the body, the individual and society. A woman's body is viewed as a biological object separate from the individual who perceives her body. It is assumed that a woman should be able to perceive her own body objectively and (more or less) accurately in the same way that she might perceive the dimensions of an inanimate object, such as a vase. Experimental procedures intensify and normalise a woman's objectifying gaze of her body through asking her to focus her gaze on her body as an object and view her body as a series of measurements. A woman is considered to be normal if she can objectively perceive the size and shape of her body consistently over time. Women's bodies can be known only through strict empirical measures of women's reported cognitive and subjective states and by body width measurements. There is no space for inconsistency, contradiction or a shifting view of one's body. The body, outside the social/cultural, is not invested with meanings, desire and an unconscious (e.g. Cash and Pruzinsky, 1990, 2002; Thompson and Smolak, 2001).

Body image discourse rests on a fundamental split between the individual and society. In experimental studies, society is operationalised as a variable influencing the minds of individual women. The notion of the individual in experimental psychology is predicated on the mind–body dualism and is constructed as objective and autonomous, a unitary, rational and consistent subject. Body image researchers take the view that something called 'societal influence' can be measured empirically and that some women are more 'susceptible' to, for example, media images of thin women, than others. Society is seen as an external force that works on the vulnerable minds of individual women.

One of the most damaging effects of body image discourse for women is that they are both blamed by society and blame themselves for their failure to resist societal influences and accept their bodies 'as they really are'. Individual explanations for women's difficulties are privileged over cultural explanations. There is no consideration that women's painful experiences of their female bodies might be culturally produced.

Body image researchers assert that women's painful feelings about their bodies are caused either by a perceptual problem – that is, women do not see their bodies 'as they really are' – or flaws in the way women think or what they feel – women have unrealistic expectations or distorted beliefs about the way their bodies look.

In this way, women's distressing experiences of their bodies are reduced simply to a concern about physical appearance.

So where does this leave Anita? Is her perception of herself faulty? As a woman in her 40s who has given birth to three children, are her expectations of what she should look like simply unrealistic? Is she particularly vulnerable to the influence of societal representations of women in their mid-40s who look much younger? Does she need to 'modify the "irrational expectations" regarding appearance that are "fostered by sociocultural factors"'? (Thompson, 1990: 105). Is her belief that her body is not acceptable due to a perceptual problem that prevents Anita from seeing her body objectively? Is it possible that Anita holds 'common irrational beliefs regarding body size, weight and overall appearance' (Thompson, Heinberg and Clarke, 2001: 314) which mean she is unable to think about her body rationally? Is Anita's dissatisfaction with her body simply all in her mind?

This book exposes the fallacies about women's bodies that underpin experimental psychology's body image research. It demonstrates the dangerous consequences of these fallacies being accepted as truths in popular texts and in the talk of 'every-day' women who have experienced distress with their bodies and eating. All of the women I spoke with had struggled with feelings of despair about their body size and shape and experienced difficulties with food. Experimental psychology has made a significant contribution to this despair.

This critique of the assumptions of experimental psychology's body image research and my argument for an alternative approach to understanding women's difficult experiences of embodiment does not, of course, constitute the 'real truth' about women's bodies. My own position is itself an historical artefact, equally contingent, that will in turn be critiqued.

The first chapter of this book provides a detailed description of experimental psychological research on body image, identifying key researchers, the psychological concepts and methods they use, and some of the assumptions underpinning their methods. A critique of this research, focusing on the potential effects of psychology's constitution of women's bodies in body image research, follows in Chapter 2. An alternative view of the body and subjectivity, as discursive products, is presented in Chapter 3. I draw upon diverse aspects of the work of Susie Orbach, Michel Foucault, Susan Bordo, Nikolas Rose, and Margaret Wetherell and Jonathan Potter's discourse analytic work to provide a theoretical framework within which to formulate an alternative understanding of many women's difficult experiences of their bodies. Quotes from women whom I interviewed about 'body image' are reproduced in these first chapters to illustrate the variety and complexity of their experiences.

In the next three chapters I model alternative ways of approaching the question of 'body image' by exploring the construction of women's bodies/subjectivities across different empirical sites. Chapters 4 and 5 focus on practices within which women's bodies are formed in particular ways. My analysis of the *More* magazine article featuring 'ordinary' women's bodies naked is the subject of a descriptive form of discourse analysis in Chapter 4. In Chapter 5 a closer reading and a more detailed analytic approach is used to examine how practices of subjectification, within body image discourse, in the broader context of popular women's magazines, produce women as having body image problems.

My interview/discussion with one woman (Emma) about 'body image' forms the basis of Chapter 6. I use a discourse analytic approach to explore how Emma's account underlines the ways in which assumptions of experimental body image research constitute her subjectivity in particular ways and discuss the effects of this constitution.

Finally, I consider the implications of my arguments for clinical practice and how, given this critical perspective, we can work with women who have difficulties with eating and who experience their bodies as a source of distress.

1
EXPERIMENTAL BODY IMAGE RESEARCH

Approaching the experimental body image literature, the sheer weight of knowledge at first seems both overwhelming and impenetrable. The experimental body image literature describes hundreds of controlled experiments, producing empirical evidence about body image and women's body image problems. A closer examination of this research reveals that its knowledge claims about women's bodies are mainly based on fundamental assumptions that are problematic for the women whom body image researchers would claim to be helping.

The phrase 'body image research' misleadingly suggests a comprehensive body of work founded on agreed-upon ontological and epistemological assumptions. In fact, definitions of body image vary greatly and stem from a range of different theoretical orientations, including phenomenology, neurology, experimental psychology, psychoanalysis and feminist philosophy. The focus of my work is on the effect of one important segment of this varied research – the use of the concept of body image in experimental psychology. My interest in this area of body image work stems from its significant social and cultural influence. I argue that scientific psychology's conceptualisation of body image and its 'disturbances' powerfully informs – indeed, *forms* – contemporary common-sense and popular understandings of the body.

The aim of this chapter is to provide a detailed description of a representative selection of experimental psychological research[1] on body image, identifying key researchers, the psychological concepts and methods they utilise, and some of the assumptions underpinning their methods. A critique of this research follows in Chapter 2, which focuses on the potential effects of psychology's constitution of women's bodies in body image research.

Historical precursors

One of the first academic psychologists to investigate body image and body perception was the North American psychologist Seymour Fisher (Fisher and Cleveland, 1958). Although only Fisher's more recent (1986) work is cited by contemporary experimental researchers, his writings about body image span four decades. Fisher's stance is an unusual mix of a psychoanalytic (Freudian) view of body image combined with a commitment to experimentally validated knowledge.

5

Fisher chastised his contemporaries from the late 1950s onwards, particularly behavioural psychologists, for only paying 'lip-service to the fact that each person is a biological object' and therefore 'regarding people as disembodied' (Fisher, 1986: xiii). For him, understanding human behaviour depended upon knowledge about 'body perception' – people's feelings and attitudes towards their bodies: 'I firmly believe we will eventually find that measures of body perception are among our most versatile predictors of how people will interpret and react to life situations' (Fisher, 1986: xii).

In 1969 Franklin Shontz, anticipating some of the themes of current research, published a series of studies about body-size judgements. He noted that generally people are less accurate in perceiving the width of their own bodies or body parts than the size of 'non-body objects'. Shontz, like Fisher, considered that the perception of body size was important to experimental psychology. Like Fisher, he also assumed the body was an object, objectively separate from the person doing the judging and able potentially to be perceived in the same way as objects that are not bodies.

Shontz asserted that there are measurable (gender-differentiated) 'patterns of over- and under-estimation' that apply to specific areas of the body. He claimed that women usually overestimate the width of their waists more than men do. He attributed this 'mistake' to women's 'concern over conforming to American standards of feminine beauty, which required a small waist as strongly as they do an ample bust' (Shontz, 1969; cited in Fisher, 1986: 163).

Prior to Fisher's work, Sidney Secord and Paul Jourard (1953), working in personality theory, emphasised 'the individual's attitudes towards his body' as being of 'crucial importance to any comprehensive theory of personality' (Secord and Jourard, 1953: 343). These researchers believed that the level of satisfaction or dissatisfaction with one's body was quantifiable as 'body-cathexis'. They produced 'The Body Cathexis Scale' in order to measure it. Almost a half century later, the scale is still used in experimental body image research to '. . . assess the more complex representations of physical appearance' (Thompson, 1990: 15). Secord and Jourard tied body cathexis to self-concept, claiming that 'valuation of the body and the self tend to be commensurate' (Secord and Jourard, 1953: 346). Low scores for body cathexis were linked with negative personality traits.

In a seminal study of body perception within experimental psychology, Traub and Orbach (1964) investigated visual perception of the physical appearance of the body. They designed an adjustable full-length mirror which could 'reflect the body of the observer on a distortion continuum ranging from extremely distorted to completely undistorted'. The task for the subject was to adjust his/her reflection until it 'appears undistorted' or '. . . so that it looks just like you'. Traub and Orbach were concerned with the distorting effects of the mind on perception, or the 'confounding of direct perception of the physical appearance of the body with those thoughts, images, attitudes and affects regarding the body' (Traub and Orbach, 1964: 65). The implicit assumption in these studies was that the mind should ideally be able to perceive the objective body more or less accurately.

There are several epistemological features of the work of these early researchers worth highlighting, since they introduce themes and a framework for understanding the notion of 'body image' which has provided the foundation for recent psychological research. The body is viewed as an object of perception objectively separate from the mind of the person doing the perceiving. It is assumed that the body can be perceived accurately or inaccurately. Failure to 'accurately' perceive one's body 'as it really is' is understood to be the result of a perceptual or cognitive disturbance within the individual. Implicit in this analysis is the idea of the norm. It is assumed that there is a 'correct' way of perceiving the body, and that failure to do so is indicative of pathology, specifically a 'disturbance' in 'body image'.

Body image disturbance and the place of perception

The work of German psychiatrist Hilde Bruch in 1962, on eating disorders, had the effect in the following decades of focusing body image research on disturbance. Bruch worked predominantly with young women diagnosed with anorexia nervosa. Her observations led her to conclude that 'What is pathognomic of anorexia nervosa is not the severity of the malnutrition *per se* . . . but rather the distortion in body image associated with it: the absence of concern about emaciation' (Bruch, 1962: 189). Bruch hypothesised an underlying perceptual 'disturbance' which meant that anorexic girls saw their 'gruesome appearance' as 'normal or right' (Bruch, 1962: 187). She asserted that there was 'a disturbance in body image of delusional proportions' present in all patients, which she regarded as an important diagnostic and prognostic sign of anorexia nervosa (Bruch, 1962: 191).

The main significance of Bruch's work for experimental body image research is her influence on researchers such as Slade and Russell. These researchers, whose work became widely cited in this field, aimed to link perception of body size with eating disorders. In 1973 they carried out a series of studies of 'the psychopathology of anorexia nervosa'. They considered the research to be important not only in establishing the diagnosis of anorexia nervosa but also in elucidating 'the pathogenesis of this puzzling illness' (Slade and Russell, 1973: 188).

Slade and Russell's emphasis on objective experimental methodology reinforced this approach as crucial to doing body image research. Twenty-five years later, others such as Thompson (1990) have been explicit:

> In recent years, attempts have been made to manipulate variables in the laboratory and measure the effects on body image indices. These laboratory models of disturbance are of critical importance to the body image field because they demonstrate with the strictest empirical controls the factors that may operate in natural settings to cause body image disturbance.
>
> (Thompson, 1990: 51–2)

As Slade and Russell's work epitomises research with such 'strict empirical controls' – an approach which has come to almost completely dominate the research area – it is worth describing their experimental method in detail.

The aim of Slade and Russell's first study (1973) was to try to measure how women with anorexia nervosa perceive their body size. Their study compared 14 anorexic patients with 20 'normal female controls', mainly postgraduate psychology students, to test the hypothesis that the anorexic patients would significantly over-estimate their size in relation to the control group. Slade and Russell's 'objective method . . . for measuring body image perception' was 'the size estimation task' (Slade and Russell, 1973: 190). This task involved the subjects estimating the width across four parts of their body; the face, the chest, the waist at the narrowest point and the hips at the widest point. These measures of 'perceived size' were obtained by a 'visual size estimation apparatus', which consisted of a movable horizontal bar mounted on a stand. Two lights attached to runners were mounted on tracks set into the horizontal bar. A pulley-device was set up so that when one of the lights was moved outwards (or inwards) from a central point, the other light moved outwards (or inwards) in the opposite direction by the same amount. At the rear of the horizontal bar a measuring instrument was attached, so that the distance between the lights could be noted. Measures of 'real size' of the women's bodies were ascertained by the use of an anthropometer – a body-measuring device. The experiments took place in a darkened experimental room and at no time was the subject informed of the results of her estimates. The measurements were obtained from the subjects while wearing their normal clothes '. . . in order to provide the most natural situation for studying body image perception' (Slade and Russell, 1973: 190).

After gathering the data from the 34 subjects, Slade and Russell devised a formula referred to as the 'body-image perception index' (BPI), which they calculated as follows:

$$\text{body image index} = \frac{\text{perceived size} \times 100}{\text{real size}}$$

Using this index, a value of 100 corresponds to 'accurate perception' of body size. A value of less than 100 shows that physical size is underestimated, and a value greater than 100 shows that physical size is overestimated.

Slade and Russell used the mean indices (BPI) for the two groups of women in this study to claim that 'while normal women tend to be remarkably accurate in their body-size estimations, patients with anorexia nervosa exhibit fairly large distortions' (Slade and Russell, 1973: 192). The authors interpreted overestimation of body width on this task as evidence of 'body image distortion'. Further, Slade and Russell noted that the four perception indices for both groups of subjects showed positive and significant intercorrelations. They claimed as a result that '. . . there is a general factor of body image perception which is observable in both anorexic patients and normals' (Slade and Russell, 1973: 191–2). Their research concretised 'body image perception' as a construct which could be both observed and measured, and could indicate some pathology.

Slade and Russell (1973: 192) also investigated the association between 'body width perception' and 'perception of non-body objects'. This experiment was based on the assumption that 'women's bodies' are a stable entity, similar to other inanimate objects. The aim of the experiment was to ascertain whether the (in)ability of individual women accurately to estimate the width of their bodies extended to estimations of the width of non-body objects. If a woman was able accurately to perceive the width of non-body objects (e.g. a vase) then her inability objectively to perceive the width of her own body could not be explained by a 'general perceptual disturbance' (Slade and Russell, 1973: 193).

According to Slade and Russell, anorexic women did not over-estimate the sizes of non-body objects (10 inch and 5 inch wooden blocks) but they 'misperceived' their own body size. Consequently, they claimed that their studies were in line with Bruch's description of body image as part of the psychopathology of anorexia nervosa. They argued that they had provided 'a simple means of identifying and measuring this perceptual disturbance'. They had offered '. . . understandings of the causation of anorexia nervosa [and] the pathological mechanisms operating in this illness' (Slade and Russell, 1973: 197).

Slade and Russell's (1973) claim to have identified 'a general factor of body image perception' and a way of measuring it encouraged further experimental research into body size perception, particularly with groups of women diagnosed as 'eating-disordered'. The notion of a 'perceptual disturbance' as the cause of 'body image disturbance' was uncritically accepted and much of the research that followed focused on inventing methods that would measure that disturbance.

Slade and Russell noted that the concept of body image was 'vague and ill-defined'. The definition they used, still in use today (see e.g. Slade, 1994), was taken from Paul Schilder, the German neuropsychologist, whom they quoted as saying that body image is 'the picture of our own body which we form in our mind, that is to say, the way in which the body appears to ourselves' (Schilder, 1935: 11; cited in Slade and Russell, 1973: 189).

Their selective use of Schilder's work omits central features of his complex, theoretical model of the body image. Schilder's conception of the body image owed more to psychoanalysis than neurophysiology. Freud's work was an important influence, in particular his conception of libidinal energy and drives. For Schilder, social and interpersonal attachments and investments, as well as libidinal energy, shape a person's self-image and conception of the body. Far from using an isolated image of the body, such as that employed by Slade and Russell (where a lone body is perceived within a 'blank' experimental space), Schilder's model involves the relations between the body, the space surrounding it, other objects and other bodies. In his model the body image 'is formed out of the various modes of contact the subject has with its environment through its actions in the world' (Grosz, 1994: 85). In 'borrowing' one aspect of Schilder's concept, Slade and Russell reduced his theory of the body image to a simple asocial mental representation of the body.

I was into all the depictions of popular culture, movies and literature. I wanted to be a lean, mean, healthy, competent machine, but also I was compelled because of my own sadness and wanting to hurt myself, what springs to mind is Heathcliff, Jane Eyre or some kind of wan heroine, romantic, I think I had that notion about that sickly part of me too. I felt quite sorry for myself and fancied myself as, and I was a bit, out on the moors alone. It didn't seem right to be healthy and hearty if that was my persona or what I identified with. It's a fine line when you tip over from being mean and lean to being sick and fragile. I even had different outfits to go with the different personas, the latest Lycra gym gear and then this long black coat I would wear.

Why did Slade and Russell adopt such a narrow and simplistic definition of body image? Schilder's complex theory of body image rested on different episte-mological and ontological assumptions, particularly in terms of the connection between the mind and body/reality, and was not amenable to experimental investigation. The assumptions of Russell and Slade and their reading of Schilder have been important in contributing to definitions of what can be said and thought about body image.

In the years since Slade and Russell (1973) established 'body image disturbance' as a construct, it has become officially recognised by the American Psychiatric Association. In 1980 it was included in the 3rd edition of the *Diagnostic and Statistical Manual of Mental Disorders*. The manual listed 'Disturbance of body image, e.g. claiming to "feel fat" even when emaciated' as the second of five neces-sary diagnostic criteria for anorexia nervosa (American Psychiatric Association, 1980: 69). Body image disturbance, operationalised as body width perception, was formally recognised as a sign of pathology, and diagnostic of anorexia nervosa.

Countless studies of body image disturbance and body size perception have followed, replicating Slade and Russell in both viewing the body as an object of perception, and assuming that its perception can and should be understood in isolation from social or 'libidinal' environments.

The experimental subjects

The subjects standing in the darkened 'experimental space' in body image research were/are most commonly women diagnosed with an eating disorder, and usually female undergraduate students (in psychology courses). Students often earn course credits for participation in experiments or, in some cases, participation is part of a research component of an introductory psychology course (see e.g. Hundleby and Bourgouin, 1993).

The accounts of experimental procedures indicate the extent to which the subjects are isolated from their social world. The following study by Norris (1984) provides a vivid account of the positioning of the women *vis-à-vis* the researcher – as simply objects of the researcher's gaze.

In a study designed to compare the 'body image' characteristics of anorexic and bulimic subjects together with two control groups, Norris (1984) used the '*mirror confrontation method*' to 'assess in each group the susceptibility of body width estimations to modification by self-inspection in a mirror and the significance of this with regard to immediate prognosis' (Norris, 1984: 836).

Norris defined body image as 'a complex phenomenon, by no means only a visually acquired experience' and argued that while '. . . self-estimation of body widths is only a very crude measure of body image . . . nevertheless, it is an easily determined and highly objective measure – a rare phenomenon in the scientific study of psychopathology' (Norris, 1984: 840).

The sample for Norris' study comprised 48 women, all under the age of 24. Twelve women were, as a result of diagnoses, assigned to one of the following four groups: 'anorexia nervosa', 'bulimia', 'emotionally disturbed females' and 'volunteer female scholars' (Norris, 1984: 836–7). Norris describes the research method as follows:

> Using an apparatus constructed to provide a continuous horizontal slit of light, instead of two separate points of light as in the Slade–Russell apparatus, perceived body widths were obtained for all subjects. The body widths chosen for estimation were all horizontal diameters readily seen on frontal silhouette; namely, the head at its widest level, the waist, the widest hip diameter, and the widest diameter of a thigh below the pubis. The experimenter located these diameters on the subject's body while naming them, but the subject was expressly forbidden to feel the widths with her hands or to observe them in any way. She was required to estimate each designated width in turn by stopping the experimenter as he slowly varied the length of the light slit. For each width four measures were taken, the experimenter alternately lengthening and shortening the slit; the average of these four readings was taken as the subject's estimate.
>
> After completion of all four estimations, the room lights were switched on and the subject, stripped semi-nude, was made to face a body-length mirror at 0.5 m distance. She was instructed to examine her body in stages from head to foot, noting her body size, running her fingers over the various fleshy and bony contours, and outlining the four estimated diameters with her hands. She was invited to describe any emotions or physical sensations provoked by this procedure. Throughout the entire experiment the tester adopted a completely neutral attitude; at no stage was the subject asked to be less defensive or more accurate; no reasons were given for the mirror confrontation; and no comments were made about her body or any feelings she expressed.
>
> The subject was then dressed and the estimation procedure was repeated in exactly the same way, but with the subject being told this time to keep

her visual and tactile impressions gained at the mirror constantly in mind as she re-estimated. Finally, real body widths were measured using anthropometric callipers.

All subjects were tested either at mid-morning or mid-afternoon, that is midway between meals, in order to minimize any possible influences of post-prandial fullness or bloatedness or pre-meal hunger. The hospitalized subjects were tested during their second week of admission, by which time any medical emergencies – such as the effects of over-dosage, severe dehydration or electrolyte disturbances – had more or less been corrected.

(Norris, 1984: 836–8)

In his discussion, Norris (1984: 840) notes that '. . . the mirror confrontation technique was designed to evaluate several aspects of the body image percept, including its stability and the emotional experience thereof which, in several cases in this study, was profound'.

There is only one study (to my knowledge) that reports on subjects' experiences of such experiments (Bullerwell-Ravar, 1996). Bullerwell-Ravar's informants described the 'mirror confrontation procedure' as 'harsh and unpleasant' (1996: 39). The above description of the semi-nude, emotional subject touching her body in front of a neutral researcher makes disturbing reading. I return to this point in detail in Chapter 2, but suffice it to say here that studies using similar methods have characterised the experimental investigation of 'body image disturbance', and measuring techniques have continued to proliferate. Whilst the 'findings' of investigations proved contradictory and inconclusive (see below), the interest in the 'physical appearance aspect' of body image intensified, particularly in relation to identifying and measuring features of eating disorders and predicting treatment outcomes.

Questions from the inside

Body image researchers after Slade and Russell have produced conflicting results. In the year following Slade and Russell's studies, British researchers Crisp and Kalucy (1974) claimed that it is not only women with anorexia nervosa who over-estimate their body size. They reported that in their study a group of 'normal females', matched for age with an 'anorexic group', also over-estimated body size, although not to the same extent as the 'anorexics'. Garner, Garfinkel, Stancer and Moldofsky (1976) claimed that 'anorexic' and 'obese' subjects over-estimated total body size, while the 'normal' subjects tended to underestimate.

It's not like I have some eating disorder but I notice I just kind of try to kid myself that I am just still my normal size 12 and then I will see a photo of myself and I will get this major shock.

12

In 1982 the construct 'body image disturbance' and its role in anorexia nervosa was challenged when Dr L. K. George Hsu reviewed the body size estimation studies that had employed 'body perception techniques' described above. Hsu (1982: 305) asked two questions: 'Do anorectics overestimate their body width and do non-anorectic females also overestimate their body width?'

In the studies reviewed by Hsu, about half of the women diagnosed as anorexic over-estimated their body width on the distorting photograph technique, while all over-estimated on the visual size estimation apparatus. Hsu then looked at the findings for the control subjects or 'non-anorectic females' in these same studies, asking whether they over-estimated body width. The majority of studies showed that 'non-anorectic' women, as well as obese and pregnant women, over-estimated their body width. He concluded that:

> Some of the normals overestimated their body width at least as much as the anorectics . . . thus, overestimation of body width cannot be held to be unique among anorectics.
>
> (Hsu, 1982: 306)

Hsu pointed out that, despite the fact that over-estimation of body width was not 'peculiar' to women with anorexia, the idea that anorectics had a disturbance in body image persisted. While Hsu agreed with fellow researchers who claimed that body perception was a valid operational measure of body image, he argued that it was problematic to equate 'claiming to feel fat despite being emaciated' with a disturbance of body image. Hsu suggested that women with anorexia nervosa may claim to feel fat despite being emaciated for a variety of reasons, such as 'equating being thin with a sense of identity, or being special or in control', and that a focus on what 'being thin' *means* to these women might be a fruitful approach to understanding their experience. Given 'the present state of our knowledge', Hsu argued, 'a "disturbance in body image" should be deleted from the diagnostic criteria for anorexia nervosa' (Hsu, 1982: 306).

What became of Hsu's argument? His 1982 paper was clearly widely read. It is cited by the key authors and numerous other researchers in the field. Nevertheless, 'body image disturbance', e.g. 'claiming to feel fat when emaciated' was one of the diagnostic criteria for anorexia nervosa in the *Diagnostic and Statistical Manual of Mental Disorders* (1980: 69) until the wording was changed for the 4th edition (American Psychiatric Association, 1994). Hsu's critical and sceptical analysis of the research field was either ignored or dismissed by those who argued that inconsistent research findings were the result of variations in subject characteristics, measurement techniques and/or experimental conditions (e.g. see reviews by Slade, 1985, below; also Cash and Brown, 1987). The position taken by researchers Ruff and Barrios (1986) exemplified the confidence in the body image construct:

> Although the body image construct has not yet proved particularly help-
> ful in explaining and predicting the course of various eating disorders,
> it nevertheless continues to surface in our writings on the origin and

treatment of maladaptive eating patterns. Such resilience suggests the concept has compelling face validity and broad base intuitive appeal that overrides its lack of empirical support.

(Ruff and Barrios, 1986: 248)

Perhaps the best evidence of Hsu's critical analysis being side-lined can be found in his later publication, written nearly ten years after the critical review. The paper by Hsu and co-author Sobkiewitz, entitled 'Body image disturbance: time to abandon the concept for eating disorders?' (1991) again questioned the utility of the concept 'body image disturbance'. Hsu and his co-author reviewed a further 19 recent studies of 'body image disturbance', only to reiterate that the findings for women with anorexia nervosa and bulimia were anything but conclusive. They observed the intransigence of the idea that over-estimation of body width is synonymous with 'body image disturbance' and pointed out the way that this 'understanding' had captured the popular imagination: '. . . even the media seemed to have caught onto this idea: the picture of an emaciated young female staring into the mirror, facing an obese image of herself, has become a popular way of depicting the illness' (Hsu and Sobkiewitz, 1991: 15–16). This compelling image is still prevalent today.

Hsu and Sobkiewitz believed it was 'unnecessary and unwarranted' to invoke the term 'body image disturbance' to explain the over-estimation of body width found in studies of patients with eating disorders. They pointed out that 'the issue of how these findings actually indicate a disturbance of body image is never addressed in these studies directly'. They questioned whether over-estimation was related to a disturbed body image, that is 'whether the former is an operational measure of the latter', and concluded that such an assumption could not be substantiated (Hsu and Sobkiewitz, 1991: 16).

For studies that measure attitude and affect towards one's body (i.e. the subjective measures of body image) Hsu and Sobkiewitz (1991: 21) noted that whilst 'body disparagement' can be defined as 'body image distortion', 'the problem is whether this is warranted'. The authors said that they '. . . are not convinced that the statement "I am dissatisfied with my body image" represents a scientific advance over the statement "I am dissatisfied with my shape/weight/how fat I feel/how big I am"' (Hsu and Sobkiewitz, 1991: 21).

Hsu and Sobkiewitz (1991: 25) were critical of the way that 'overestimation of body size' and 'disturbance of body image' had been used interchangeably. They asked, 'What does overestimation mean? If overestimation occurs in only a proportion of anorexics and bulimics as well as in some normal controls, it cannot be pathognomonic of the eating disorders. This finding is "non-specific"' (Hsu and Sobkiewitz, 1991: 26). The authors concluded that the construct of 'body image disturbance . . . has generated little meaningful research in the past 16 years and is unlikely, in our view, to do so in the foreseeable future. Furthermore, the term creates confusion both in the mind of the public and in our own, it suggests progress where there is none' (Hsu and Sobkiewitz, 1991: 28).

In stark contrast to Hsu's (1982) review of studies, Slade (1985) illustrates, in a review of body image studies in anorexia nervosa, an ongoing confidence in the paradigm shared by many researchers at the time, and to this day. In an innovative statistical reworking of the data from a group of 'body perception' studies, Slade, who does not acknowledge Hsu's (1982) review and critical analysis, produced the following account of psychological knowledge about 'body image disturbance':

> Since the publication of our paper in 1973 there have been many reports of studies attempting to replicate and extend these findings . . . this paper has been cited over 80 times in the scientific literature over the past ten years, indicating the apparent popularity of the area as a subject for enquiry and discussion. Many of the attempts to replicate or extend our findings have produced inconsistent or theoretically more complex results. However, what is clear is that these contributions have been of a generally high standard and have helped to put our original experimental results into a wider and more realistic perspective.
>
> (Slade, 1985: 256)

In an attempt to make some conclusive comments about these 'inconsistent or theoretically more complex results' Slade employed two different analyses. First, he compared groups of women across studies by using averaged Body Perception Index values for anorexic and comparison groups.[2] Next, he compared the number of over-estimators (of body width) and also the number of studies producing significant vs. non-significant group comparisons. This analysis (using t-tests) led Slade to conclude that 'while both anorexics and controls over-estimated their body widths, on average, the anorexics did so to a significantly greater degree than controls ($t = 2.60$, p [more] 0.05)' (Slade, 1985: 257).

Slade suggested that all the experimental procedures for assessing body image 'measure a similar aspect of the problem' but that their sensitivity in identifying 'distortion tendencies' differs (Slade, 1985: 263). He thought that size-estimation methods have lower thresholds for identifying over-estimation tendencies than image-distorting methods. The former procedures, he argued, lead to more anorexics and more non-anorexics over-estimating their body size.

Slade also thought that the differences in findings, using different instruments, may be qualitative as well as quantitative. He suggested that 'the two sets of procedures measure different (but related) aspects of body image' (Slade, 1985: 263). Employing a familiar distinction in attitudinal and psychometric research between cognition and affect, Slade argued that errors of over-estimation recorded by the image-distorting techniques reflect '. . . a relatively fixed, cognitive attitude to body size which in anorexics has all the hallmarks of an irrational (if not a delusional) belief' (Slade, 1985: 263). Errors in estimation using the 'size-estimation procedure' in contrast '. . . reflect a fluid state of body size sensitivity, which is strongly influenced by affective/emotional factors and which is responsive to changes in both the external and the internal environment' (Slade, 1985: 264).

This distinction between cognition or rationality, and affect or emotion, typifies much of the contemporary 'body image' literature, with researchers claiming to be able to discern the two as separate. The implication is also that one causally affects the other – that is, a woman's emotion renders her irrational. Emotion is the source of error. Such claims have important effects on women's subjectivities as constituted within body image knowledge, and on possible understandings of (women's) experiences of embodiment (see Chapter 2).

Body image dissatisfaction – the place of cognition

Measurement of the 'subjective component' of body image signalled in the early work of Secord and Jourard (1953) above, and mentioned in passing by Slade in his 1985 review, received much less attention than the 'perceptual component' so central in 'body image disturbance'. Research into the 'subjective component' primarily uses written questionnaires to elicit and measure attitudes and affect, including dissatisfaction with body size/shape and fear of obesity. This type of measurement is concerned with attitudes which are seen as linked to the cognitive representation of positive or negative aspects of the body.

One of the most commonly used methods utilises schematic figures or silhouettes of different body sizes. Subjects choose the two figures they think reflect their current and their ideal body size. The discrepancy between the size/shape of these two measures is taken as an indication of the subject's level of dissatisfaction with her body (Thompson, Penner and Altabe, 1990; see also Fallon and Rozin, 1985).

Thomas Cash has been an important researcher in centring attitudes as important to understanding body image. Cash and Henry (1995) defined body image attitudes as consisting of 'self-perceptions, cognitions, affect, and behaviors vis-à-vis one's physical attributes. As a salient feature of self-concept, body image bears a moderate relationship to self-esteem and psychosocial adjustment (e.g. eating disturbances, depression, social anxiety, and sexual functioning)' (Cash and Henry, 1995: 19; see also Cash, 2002b; Cash and Pruzinsky, 1990; Thompson, 1990).

Using the same sorts of methods from the perceptual studies, Cash and his colleagues developed a 'mirror focus procedure' which they claim measures the affective component of dissatisfaction (Butters and Cash, 1987). This method requires subjects to examine all their body features as they gaze into a full-length tri-fold mirror, for 30 seconds at a distance of 3 feet. Following this, subjects are asked to rate their comfort–discomfort level on a subjective units-of-distress scale from 0 (absolute calm) to 100 (extreme discomfort).

More recent innovations in method include a new 'mirror-based assessment method' for measuring body size perception (Farrell, Shafron and Fairburn, 2003) and a computer program for measuring 'body size distortion and body satisfaction'

> When I am feeling like I don't really care what size I am and I'm enjoying my life and I'm okay the way I am, then I don't think about being over-weight. It's just not an issue. It comes and goes and I'll be thinking, 'Oh that's fantastic, I've got this huge burden off me', and I'm not worried about it, you know? And I go out and do my stuff and wear whatever clothes I've got.

(Gardner and Boice, 2004). As well as these techniques, the ever-expanding body image literature contains a fast-growing assortment of questionnaires purportedly measuring some new aspect of subjective dissatisfaction. One such popular instrument is the *Body Parts Satisfaction Scale* (BPSS), which lists 24 body parts that are rated, by the subject, on a scale ranging from extremely dissatisfied to extremely satisfied (Berscheid, Walster and Bohrnstedt, 1973; Petrie, Tripp and Harvey, 2002). The *Body Shape Questionnaire* claims to measure concerns about body shape (Cooper, Taylor, Cooper and Fairburn, 1987), while the *Body Image Avoidance Questionnaire* (Rosen, Srebnik, Saltzburg and Wendt, 1991) is a self-report technique designed to measure behavioural tendencies which, the authors claim, frequently accompany body image disturbance. Questionnaires asking subjects to rate the frequency and content of their cognitions include one developed by Schulman, Kinder, Powers, Prange and Cleghorn (1986), the *Bulimia Cognitive Distortions Scale* (BCDS). Examples of items include: 'My value as a person is related to my weight' and 'If my hair isn't perfect I'll look terrible'. Cash, Winstead and Janda (1986) invented the *Body Self-Relations Questionnaire* (BSRQ), which has three attitudinal subscales, evaluation, attention/importance and behaviour, for each of three 'somatic domains', appearance, fitness and health. Sample items include, 'I like my looks just the way they are' and 'I am physically unattractive'.

Cash and Labarge (1996) developed a new 'cognitive body image assessment' called *The Appearance Schemas Inventory*. This 14-item scale has been designed to assess core beliefs or assumptions about the importance, meaning and effects of appearance in one's life. Sample items from the Personal Opinions Questionnaire, which is part of this inventory, include 'Attractive people have it all' and 'Homely people have a hard time finding happiness' (Cash and Labarge, 1996: 47–8). This tool has recently been extensively revised to improve the assessment of 'body image investment' (see Cash, Melnyk and Hrabosky, 2004). *The Body Image Quality of Life Inventory* (BIQLI) has been developed 'to measure the impact of body-image experiences' (Cash and Fleming 2002).

The questionnaires and scales are designed to 'tap into' and describe cognitive processes. These tools do not collect qualitative data. They are typically 'forced-choice' questions, with possible answers provided. They only permit certain – predetermined – responses.

Popularising of 'body image' dissatisfaction/disturbance

In contrast to most academic research, which remains well within the preserves of academic journals, experimental research on body image dissatisfaction has caught wide public attention via popular publications, such as *Psychology Today*, and, of course, women's magazines. Information about 'body image problems' is disseminated in *Psychology Today* via authoritative reporting of 'findings' and 'facts', as well as appeals to common-sense understandings about women's dissatisfaction with their bodies (e.g. see discussion of editorial, below). Unlike the prescriptions for other research publications, references are not included with the articles in *Psychology Today*.

Psychology Today has played a significant role not only in disseminating body image research but also in collecting research data. Over the past 14 years, large-sample reader surveys have been conducted under the authorship of prestigious researchers, such as Cash *et al*. (1986) and Garner and Kearney-Cooke (1997). These surveys utilise items from psychometric questionnaires, such as those described above, to elicit 'knowledge' from readers about their 'body image'. Responses to these surveys are interpreted, scored and analysed statistically by researchers, who then reproduce these 'findings' in *Psychology Today* as 'facts' about 'body image dissatisfaction and/or disturbance', and 'results' that provide evidence of women's negative body image attitudes.

The format of these surveys typically includes an editorial which introduces the reader to the topic of 'body image', and provides information about 'body image' and 'body image problems'. In the 1996 survey, readers are told:

> For as long as anyone's been counting – at least three decades – women have been at war with their bodies. Dissatisfied with their appearance and wanting to lose weight, they have often gone to extremes to do so . . .
> (Garner and Kearney-Cooke, 1997: 55)

The following definition of body image is provided for *Psychology Today* readers:

> Body image is a complex and puzzling topic; one that has fascinated psychologists and neurologists for many years. It is a term that almost everyone seems to grasp but even experts do not really understand. It is concerned not only with external and objective attributes but also with subjective representations of physical appearance: beliefs, feelings, sensations, and perceptions about the body. Most of the information on body image is based on clinical populations, women (and some men) with serious psychological disorders, such as anorexia and bulimia nervosa, or people with physical deformities. However, everyone has a body image and it has strong emotional overtones based on our experiences in life. Our image of our body plays a major role in how we feel, what we do,

18

whom we meet, whom we marry, and what career path we choose, even if its precise meaning and its role in mental well-being continue to elude psychologists.

(Garner and Kearney-Cooke, 1997: 56)

From Garner's definition it is evident that the concept of body image has extended and concretised to become a concept that names something that everyone 'has' – something that is measurable and about which truths can be 'found'. It is also clearly something which is, or should be, important to every person because it plays a major part in everyone's (most notably women's) significant life events.

The 1996 *Psychology Today* survey that follows Garner's introduction to body image is a 64-point questionnaire with limited-choice answers. The reader must choose one of a set of possible responses. Items include: 'How do you feel about your body?'; 'What causes negative feelings about your body?'; 'What causes positive feelings about your body?'; 'How many calories do you think you consume each day?'; and 'If I could weigh exactly what I want for the rest of my life, I would trade how many months/years of my life?' Response choices for this latter question range from '1 month' to 'more than 5 years'. Interestingly, 'none' is not an option.

The 'results' of this survey were published as an authoritative psychological report on body image in a popular Australian women's magazine, *New Woman* (1997). I will return to this in Chapter 5, where I focus on how 'body image discourse' disseminated via popular journals and women's magazines mediates and produces women's self-understandings of their bodies and subjectivities.

The use of the popular, academic journal *Psychology Today* to disseminate and collect data, as well as educate the public about body image, illustrates an important aspect of the interpenetration of academic and popular discourses on body image. This merging of experimental psychology and the popular has a powerfully self-sustaining effect on body image as a construct. The research on body image and its disturbance provides an authoritative, scientific, framework within which women can give meaning to their experiences – including their experiences of their bodies, which are scientifically formulated as problematic. 'Knowledge' about body image – what it is, and why we should know about it, the role it plays in our lives, the language associated with 'talk' about body image, all of this provides women with a way of thinking about their bodies and experiencing embodiment.

Although presented as exposing the objective 'truth' about a pre-existing factor called 'body image', the body image 'findings' and questionnaires are themselves *tools of production of body image*. The surveys assume the existence of body image, and its measurability. Meaning is singular – body image is a fixed characteristic which all of us 'have'. The forced-choice questions elicit particular responses and rule out or suppress others. The responses inevitably are going to fit within the assumptions and the 'knowledge' already produced within the theoretical frames of the researchers in their laboratories, and will necessarily reinforce those findings. In this way, body image researchers *are simply describing their own production*.

This point is developed further in this book as I discuss the relationship between experimental psychology's (manufacture of) body image and many women's daily (problematic) experience of embodiment. In a perfectly circular way, this experience is then identified by experimental psychologists as body image dissatisfaction, or disturbance.

The 'spread' of body image dissatisfaction to the 'normal' population

It is hardly surprising, if we follow the argument above, that body image problems are becoming more and more common. This final section examines research published in the 'Body Image' issue of *Psychology Today* (Thompson, 1986), which reports on the worrying spread of body image disturbance. In the report, J. Kevin Thompson indicates that experimental research on 'the physical aspect of body image' has proliferated over the last 10 years and extended investigations to larger populations of 'normal' women and girls. Thompson explains his rationale for focusing 'body image' investigations on 'normal' women.

> Cathy also stands in front of the mirror each morning, but she tries various combinations of skirts and blouses to reduce the apparent size of her stomach. Although no one agrees with her, she can't get over the feeling that her paunch protrudes, making her look 3 months pregnant. Her midsection continues to haunt her but she has never forced herself to throw up after eating.
>
> For the past few years, however, I have devoted most of my research on body perception to women like Cathy who do not have eating disorders but seem to have unwarranted concern about the size of a particular body part. I started by taking advantage of the fact that most previous studies on perception of body size involving anorexics and bulimics almost always included a control group of women without any easily recognisable eating disorder symptoms.
>
> The researchers in these studies, such as David Garner at the University of Toronto, typically have found that women with eating disorders have distorted self-images. When I re-examined these studies, I found that, on average, the normal women also overestimated their body size. In fact several studies found no difference between the body size distortions of anorexic and normal women.

Thompson extended his research to women who have no symptoms of eating disorders. He reported that he and his colleagues tested more than 100 women free of eating disorder symptoms and 95% of the women over-estimated their body size – on average one-fourth larger than they really were.

> Why do people, especially women, have distorted body images? [asks Thompson]. There are at least two rival theories. Some researchers believe

20

that distortion results from a perceptual defect: people who over-estimate body size may have a visual–spatial problem in brain function that interferes with accurate perception. Other researchers think that the problem is emotional or cognitive. Size judgements are determined largely by what people feel or think about their bodies.

(Thompson, 1986: 42)

These theories were 'tested' by Thompson and Dolce and published in the *Psychology Today* report (no reference given). A group of 34 women were asked to estimate the size of their cheeks, waist, hips and thighs, using two different sets of instructions. The subjects '. . . were told to first rate themselves on the basis of a logical rational assessment of the facts' and secondly to rate themselves 'based on what you feel about your body at this moment'. The authors reported:

If there had been a difference between the ratings, we would have suspected an emotional or cognitive problem. But since there was no real difference for most of the women between the two sets of ratings, we believe that in their case a perceptual defect may have prevented them from describing themselves accurately. We are trying to nail down this connection more carefully by using specific visual and neuropsychological tests. About a quarter of the women, however, made radically different estimations of body size in the two sets of ratings. For them, the inaccuracy seemed to be based on their feelings rather than their physical problems in perception.

(Thompson and Dolce, reproduced in Thompson, 1986)

Thompson, along with most of his fellow researchers, assumes first of all that body image disturbance exists. He then implies that, because 'normal' women as well as women with eating disorders over-estimate body size, these 'normal' women also exhibit evidence of a pathology, that is, they have 'body image disturbance'. On the basis of his conclusions, Thompson and others have extended their experimental investigations of 'body image disturbance' and 'body image dissatisfaction' to larger and larger groups of 'normal' women and girls (Thompson, 1986: 39–40). In no time at all, there is an epidemic of 'disturbed' women.

Not only is disturbance widespread, but most women are 'asymptomatic' because, although they exhibit the classic signs of body image disturbance, they are not anorexic. In his guide for psychology practitioners on 'body image disturbance', Thompson (1990) observed that the investigation of 'the subjective component' of body image in 'normal populations' of adult women has become so commonplace that there are now '. . . more studies with asymptomatic subjects' subjective disturbance than with the subjective dysfunction of individuals with anorexia nervosa or bulimia nervosa' (1990: 30). Further, Thompson claims that: '. . . this group (of normal women) appears to be at greatest risk . . . there is now general agreement that a large degree of dysfunction exists, particularly in the areas of subjective happiness with body size, weight, and appearance' (1990: 9).

On the basis of research studies such as those he conducted and his interpretation of earlier research studies, described above, Thompson concludes:

> . . . it is apparent that serious, clinically relevant body image dysfunction now exists in non-eating-disordered populations.
>
> (Thompson, 1990: 23)

Recent research on women's body image and weight perceptions points to an increase in women's dissatisfaction with their bodies (see e.g. Feingold and Mazzella, 1998; Grogan, 1999). As the experimental literature on 'body image' has grown over the past 40 years, so has body image dysfunction in the population. Interestingly, and alarmingly, the relationship between these phenomena seems to have gone unnoticed by the researchers. In the next chapter, I consider this productive relationship, and how body image researchers, using an objectivist framework, are precluded from awareness of the social and constitutive effects of their research assumptions.

Notes

1. The term 'experimental' research refers to both experimental and cognitive studies in psychology's body image research.
2. It is noteworthy that Slade excluded two of the nine available studies from his data analysis. He addressed this in a footnote: 'The two studies which had to be excluded were those of Crisp and Kalucy (1974) and Garner et al. (1976), both of which produced negative results. However, it is unlikely that their exclusion will affect the overall conclusions, given the small numbers involved' (Slade, 1985: 257). This means that the two studies omitted showed a result in the reverse direction, for example, Garner et al. (1976: 330) found that 'all groups over-estimated all four body regions'. Such an omission can change the result of a statistical test and there is a strong possibility that had all the data been included the result, and therefore the conclusion, would have been different. Slade does not offer an acceptable rationale for dropping these two groups, neither does he demonstrate that it did not affect the results.

2
CRITIQUE OF BODY IMAGE RESEARCH

'Body image' research is alive and well and clearly established within the mainstream psychological literature. Researchers claim to have discovered and identified a psychological construct called 'body image disturbance', also referred to as 'body image dissatisfaction'. They claim to be able objectively to measure 'body image disturbance' using specifically-designed scientific methods and instruments. The purpose of these research studies is to accumulate knowledge that will enable the researchers to identify, explain, predict and treat the 'body image disturbance' they themselves have conceptualised and measured. In their introduction to *Body Image, Eating Disorders, and Obesity in Youth: Assessment, Prevention and Treatment* (2001), J. Kevin Thompson and co-editor Linda Smolak note that this research is growing at 'a fast and furious pace'.

This chapter shifts from the description of experimental body image research (in Chapter 1) to a more detailed critique of it. Here I will analyse the fundamental assumptions that underlie body image research, with reference to the work of critical social psychologists and social constructionists. My analysis, and that of these critical theorists, show that, due to their narrow focus on a pre-existing, measurable reality, traditional body image researchers fail to understand their findings as social products rather than 'objective descriptions of reality'. The 'findings' of body image researchers then go on to have major – and, I will argue, damaging – social implications for women's lives, in particular, the ways women can experience embodiment.

The mind–body dualism

A key underlying assumption of body image research concerns the relation between mind and body. This relationship is understood in terms of 'perception' – the more, or less, accurate apprehension by the individual's mind of an external reality, in this case, the (her) body.

Any study of body image necessarily involves some theory of 'the body' – what it is and how we might understand its role in human behaviour. The psychological construct of 'body image' is built on assumptions about the body and its relationship to the mind. Psychological theory and practice rests on the ontological assumption of a mind–body opposition. Based on the Cartesian system of binaries that structures language and underpins Western thought, the mind is separated from the body in a hierarchical way (characteristic of other dualist ontologies, such as the opposition of male and female, culture and nature, and reason and emotion).

The mind separate from the body is the source of meaning, and knowledge about the body. The body becomes simply an object of this knowledge, rather than its effect. Separate from the mind, the body and its social experiences are relevant to knowledge only insofar as they can be scientifically measured as 'objects'. Fisher and Cleveland's (1958) and Shontz's (1969) work, in conceptualising the body as a 'biological object' and an object similar to other 'non-body objects' , epitomised this binary (see Chapter 1).

The way psychology has negotiated this dualism has been to create a relation between the two entities, mind and body, via the notion of perception. Perception is held to be the connection between the two, where the body is reduced to what the individual's mind can see, think and say about it (Grosz, 1994). The perceptive mind or consciousness, therefore, is taken as the object of investigation and the body relegated to the status of a physical object – the object of perception. Through its exclusion from concepts of subjectivity or identity, 'the body becomes an "objective" observable entity, a thing' (Grosz, 1987: 8).

> It was the same every morning when I woke up, I'd sort of feel okay then I'd remember. This thing, this heavy thing. I would lift my head up off the pillow and look at it, lying there, hating it. It was as if that fleshy body, ugly and all wrong, was dragging me down.

As the body is merely an object of perception, it is implicitly constructed as pre-discursive, the 'natural' body outside the social/cultural. In mainstream psychological body image research, the body is not invested with meanings, desire and an unconscious. This view is contested by contemporary critical social psychologists, philosophers, feminist theorists and social theorists (e.g. Bordo, 1993a, 1993b; Butler, 1990; Malson, 1998; Ussher, 1997a, 1997b).

Perception as cognitive work

Psychology's body image research has a particular view of perception in its form-ulation 'body image disturbance'. A claim that characterises social, developmental and mainstream psychology is that internal cognitive processes of individuals are central to informing perception and action. It is claimed that cognitive representations (e.g. mental picture of one's body shape) are perceptually based and that perception is essentially realistic, i.e. potentially an accurate representation of the measurable, pre-existing, external reality. The fundamental proposition is that an individual's information-processing procedures – thought – can accurately represent external reality. In its most empiricist form, representation theory conceptualises the relation between thought and reality as a correspondence (Henriques, Hollway, Urwin, Venn and Walkerdine, 1984).

The central belief is that it is possible to apprehend 'reality' on the basis of what we can see with our own eyes. A pervasive visualism underpins perception, privileging sensory input as the route to (more or less accurate) knowledge of the world. Slade states that 'body image' might be defined as 'the picture we have in our minds of the size, shape and form of our bodies . . .' (Slade, 1994: 497). This picture is supposed to come directly from our visual apprehension of our real bodies. Because perception is held to be basically realistic, this 'picture we have in our minds' is, ideally, an accurate representation of our body, 'as it really is'.

> Sometimes I love my body, sometimes I forget all about it, sometimes I'm disappointed or impatient because I'm not thin and ethereal looking. I think the best way to describe how I am with my body are the words from Phoebe Snow's song, "Sometimes these hands are so clumsy that I drop things and people laugh, sometimes these hands have so much class I can see them signing autographs". I feel like that about my body, different feelings at different times.

An ideal of clear and unimpeded perception – of our bodies – is assumed not only to be possible, but also to be the healthy norm. The perceptual model assumes that 'correct' or rational and objective information processing will result in accurate perception and representation (Henriques *et al.*, 1984). Although experimental psychology is compatible with a variety of epistemological stances, overwhelmingly simple realism forms the backdrop, implicitly and explicitly, to experimental research. The world is viewed as stable and unchanging, comprised of solid physical objects. The belief that perception can be *either* veridical, a true representation of a real world, *or* incorrect reflects this assumption. The object of perception, in this case the body, is taken to be a stable, real object 'out there' – not a constructed object, but a natural object with real properties which are amenable to accurate or inaccurate perception. This ideal is implicit in the laboratory experiments described in the previous chapter and is formalised explicitly in Slade and Russell's 'Body Perception Index' (see Chapter 1).

A 'healthy, normal' woman is expected to be able 'accurately' (as defined by the experimenter) to perceive her body width. Inaccuracy (a score less or greater than 100) signals deviation from the norm, i.e. 'disturbance'. The causes of this disturbance, or misperception, then become the focus of experimental investigations. In body image studies, 'misperception of body size and shape is the central concern' (Slade, 1994: 497).

Causal mechanisms – explanations for misperception

Because all human behaviour is held to be the consequence of identifiable causal mechanisms, the main focus of traditional experimental research is a search for causal laws. Body image disturbance is believed to be 'caused' by perceptual or cognitive 'distortions'; '. . . [body image] distortion results from a perceptual defect: people who over-estimate body size may have a visual–spatial problem in brain function that interferes with accurate perception' (Thompson, 1986: 42). If there is no evidence of a 'visual–spatial problem', then researchers claim that the cause of the 'disturbance' is an emotional or cognitive problem 'determined largely by what people feel or think about their bodies' (Thompson, 1986: 42).

According to traditional or scientific psychology, the 'cause' of body image misperception or disturbance is within 'psychologically real cognitive structures'. One such mental structure used by cognitive, social and developmental psychology is the 'schema'. The schema is 'a hypothetical cognitive organisation' with the role of making sense of experience and guiding our actions in the world. Schemas enable people in everyday situations 'to see the world for what it is'. A schema is 'a spatially and/or temporally organised cognitive structure in which the parts are connected on the basis of contiguities that have been experienced in time or space' (Mandler, 1979: 263).

Because cognitive schemas are considered central to understanding body image disturbance, researchers have invented a plethora of diagnostic scales and questionnaires for measuring cognitive events that are effects of these schemas. The Bulimia Cognitive Distortions Scale (BCDS) (Schulman et al., 1986) and The Appearance Schemas Inventory (ASI) (Cash and Labarge, 1996; Cash, Melnyk and Hrabosky, 2004) are two examples (others are listed in Chapter 1). The latter scale, claim the authors, assesses core beliefs or assumptions about the 'importance, meaning, and effects of appearance in one's life' (Cash and Labarge, 1996: 37). It relies on the notion of the 'schema' or 'self-schema', which they describe (following Beck and Freeman, 1990) as 'cognitive structures that organize experience and action . . . their content is reflected in implicit rules, attitudes, beliefs and assumptions that determine the substance of thought, emotion, and behaviour' (Cash and Labarge, 1996: 38). Schemas influence the processing of information about the self 'in a number of domains including personality, sex-role identity, the social self, and body weight/shape/appearance' (Cash and Labarge, 1996: 38).

Schemas offer specific explanations for body image problems. Researchers argue that some people are 'schematic for physical appearance'. These people are more reactive to 'stimuli' related to the schema for 'physical appearance'.

> . . . someone who is schematic for some dimension of the self will process information relevant to that dimension differently than someone who is aschematic for the dimension. For example, a person schematic for physical appearance would encode, process, and react to a wide variety of appearance-related stimuli. A magazine at the newsstand that proclaims

'Fail-Safe Beauty Makeovers!' may be more readily noticed. The sight of a cookie jar might trigger thoughts of weight gain.

(Cash and Labarge, 1996: 38)

The researchers maintain that 'appearance-schematic-individuals' are more focused on their appearance than 'normal' people, and this has emotional effects:

> . . . appearance-schematic-individuals are more psychologically invested in their looks as a standard of self-evaluation and index of self-worth. Self-schemas are also affect-laden. For example, among persons schematic for body weight, exposure to negative body weight information would provoke increased body image dissatisfaction and dysphoria.
>
> (Altabe and Thompson, 1996: 178)

Appearance schemas are measured through answers to questions on the ASI (Cash and Labarge, 1996; Cash, Melnyk and Hrabosky, 2004). This inventory indicates 'core self-representations *vis-à-vis* physical appearance', which 'may exist as cognitive structures of varying availability and accessibility'. The ASI gives access to 'underlying, affect-laden cognitive constructs' that mediate information processing.

My father frequently made disparaging comments about my body and commented on what I ate. When I was a child he would say I was too skinny, then after puberty, even though I was still thin, he called me fat. He would say things like, 'the only exercise you need is to push yourself away from the dinner table'. He used to say, and I still find this really upsetting, that no-one would want to be my friend if I was fat.

While cognitive constructs might be 'affect-laden', researchers claim to be able to make a distinction between cognition and affect (see e.g. Slade, 1985, in Chapter 1). Affect, or emotion, is considered to be a cause of much body image disturbance. It is believed that people can think rationally (correctly) about their body size, without the distorting interference of emotion. In one study, researchers investigating body width perception were first asked to estimate their body width 'on the basis of a logical rational assessment of the facts', and then according to 'what you feel about your body at this moment' (Thompson and Dolce, cited in Thompson, 1986: 42). When some women over-estimated their body width when reporting what they 'felt' but not when reporting what they 'thought', this was considered to show that 'the inaccuracy was based on their feelings' (Thompson, 1986: 43). The cause of 'disturbance' was an emotional problem rather than a cognitive one.

Underlying this distinction between emotion and rationality is the ideal of a non-contradictory, rational subject. This ideal is the implicit norm against which all 'deviations' are measured. Any responses or behaviours that fall outside of what is considered to be the rational ideal are taken to be 'distortions' or 'errors' in cognitive and perceptual processes. By dichotomising 'thought' and 'feeling' (rationality and emotion), researchers can conclude that one cause of 'body image disturbance' is a failure of individual rationality. By implication, the body image-disturbed person is irrational.

In summary, underpinning this research are clear assumptions on which the whole notion of body image and body image disturbance rests. First, there is an objectively knowable body which can be perceived more or less accurately (body image) by the more or less rational mind. Second, hypothetical 'real' cognitive structures – whose output can be measured – are considered to be the site of inaccurate perception.

Body image research is thus characterised by a strongly objectivist framework. Objectivism assumes an ontologically given external world, which is made up of entities 'with fixed properties and relations holding amongst them at any instant' (Lakoff, 1987: 162). The ideal or normal mind functions as a mirror of nature; correct, consistent, mental representations get their meaning via the extent of their correspondence with things in the world and are seen as ideally reflecting external reality. It is these epistemological assumptions, and the ontological ones that accompany them (above), which form the basis for the critique of the work of body image researchers.

Counter-positions

Rather than assuming an ontologically-given external world that is more or less stable, critics argue instead that the world is shifting and changing, comprised of 'social facts' rather than 'sensory facts' (Wetherell and Potter, 1992: 42). On this social constructionist approach, the person, body, world are not fixed entities that can be objectively or accurately described, but are held to be 'a continuously changing and fluid history of relationships' (Gergen, 1985, 1991, 1994). Bruner (1990: 107) has argued that 'the person is best understood not as the pure and enduring nucleus but [as] the sum and swarm of participations in social life'. From this perspective, there is no 'true self' waiting to be discovered. Instead, identity is held to be multi-faceted; there are a number of 'contextual selves' (Wetherell and Maybin, 1995) – the people we are in different social–relational settings.

This alternative discourse produces a different body/subjectivity from that of traditional psychology, which has significant implications for the notion of 'body image'. Crucially, this perspective highlights the productive aspects of discourse. Academic and popular discourses can be understood as sites of production and sites of struggle over the multiplicity of meanings of the body/subjectivity and experience.

Social constructionist ideas and practices emphasise the social and relational constitution of knowledge (Gergen, 1994). They argue against the individual–society dualism and for an integrated view of the person and his/her social context. With the distinction between the person and the social context denied, the mind, consciousness and self are viewed as thoroughly social. That is, how someone thinks about him/herself – or reality – can only be 'made up' from the cultural beliefs and meanings available at any historical moment.

Most social constructionists take a relativist position which foregrounds difference and diversity rather than universal standards of judgement. Attention is paid to who sees and how they see. Differences amongst and between people are taken into account in terms of the various ways that they comprehend experience and give meaning to objects, events and processes in their social world. From this perspective, objects in the world (in this case the body) are seen as the consequence of generations of human praxis (theory and action), as intensely worked over and worked up as part of historical practices.

From this perspective, the concept of 'body image' and its disturbances can be seen as specific socio-historic productions. Researchers' claims that scientific findings reveal the 'truth' about women's bodies/subjectivities can be seen as partial (in both senses of the word). Stories manufactured from beliefs, theories and language are used and legitimated in their field of expertise.

> When I hear myself talking to you about all this body image stuff now, I think, I didn't used to think about this so much or talk about it like this before. I think if it hadn't been for reading about it in magazines I wouldn't have given it that much thought.

Social constructionism is a language-based approach to knowledge which takes a view, different from that of experimental psychology, of how language is used to communicate meaning within a culture. From this perspective, language does not get its meaning via a correspondence with objects or events in the external world, neither is it seen as expressing or reflecting already existing psychological and social realities. Instead, language is taken to be constitutive of social life and social practices. Language 'makes things happen' – that is, it is used to construct and create social interaction and diverse social worlds (Wetherell and Potter, 1992: 101–15). Language, in this view, is an activity that is both performative and indexical. The meaning and relevance of expressions are determined by the context and occasions in which they are used (Barnes and Law, 1976).

Theorising the (psychological) individual

Knowledge about 'body image disturbance' relies on assumptions about the nature of human beings and how we can understand human behaviour. A particular individual is the imagined body/subject of body image discourse. This notion of the individual, predicated on a mind–body dualism, powerfully shapes the way that 'body image' is conceptualised and hence how women's bodies/subjectivities are reproduced as pathological within body image research.

As outlined above, the ontological assumption of a mind–body dualism privileges the mind and rational consciousness over the passive object of the body, the denigrated term in the binary. The 'self' that is the Enlightenment individual is constructed as objective and autonomous, a unitary, rational and consistent subject. She/he is considered to be unique and self-contained, quite separate from other people. The individual is conceptualised as having her/his own private inner world of thoughts and feelings. These are self-generated internal states that can be 'given voice' publicly through language or actions. It is taken for granted that language is transparent and an individual's words more or less accurately reflect her/his inner world of thoughts and feelings (Wetherell and Maybin, 1995). The individual is thus an asocial, rational being, privileged as the source of consciousness, truth and knowledge, rather than being produced by/in the world. She/he is taken to be the initiator of action and the origin of her/his own desires and beliefs. These ideas inform common-sense understandings of the individual or 'self' of Western thought as she/he is conceptualised in psychology and in everyday talk.

The notion of the individual as it is used explicitly and implicitly within body image research rests on a clear demarcation between the individual and the social context. This individualistic concept of self, contrary to alternative theories of subjectivity as socially produced, privileges individual, cognitive explanations for action at the expense of social and cultural understandings (see e.g. Henriques, Hollway, Urwin, Venn and Walkerdine, 1984; Gergen, 1985; Potter and Wetherell, 1987).

What got me every time about being heavy was people saying things like, 'But you've got such a pretty face!' Of course, the implication was if that bit was okay then potentially the rest of my body could follow. I used to believe there was a thin me struggling to get out of this misshapen, oversized body. I was such a sucker for the idea that within every fat woman is a thin woman waiting to get out. Then I'd show them all. The real me would emerge. She would be fantastic – and thin.

Traditionally, cognitive, social and developmental psychology has insisted that some notion of the individual can be found inside the body, in the form of traits, attitudes, drives or mechanisms instead of in the context of people's social relationships (Radley, 1991). The 'individual' is seen as amenable to psychological investigation. It is posited that some essential self resides 'within' the individual that can be uncovered and the individual can be known, measured and described. Within traditional or mainstream psychological research, it is taken for granted that 'truths' about individuals and their behaviour can be obtained through the correct use of scientific methods.

Historically, the focus of traditional psychology has been on pathology, specifically on defining and identifying deviance and, therefore, establishing what is considered to be 'normal'. The belief in a unitary, rational self and a goal of achieving coherence, consistency and rationality underpins notions of 'normality'. This concept of normality leaves no discursive space for inconsistency, contradictions, ambivalence or multiplicity. For example, researchers maintain that 'body image' is a real, stable psychological construct and more or less consistent over time. In some experimental studies, where women varied their estimations of body width over time they were deemed to have either 'weak' or 'unstable' body images (see Slade, 1994).

Trait theory

An example of a psychological approach which assumes (and produces) a 'real, stable' self is trait theory. Trait theory has been extremely influential, particularly within social psychology. The self is conceptualised as having fixed, measurable personality traits, abilities and attributes. Personality traits are viewed as stable and consistent over time and more or less permanent. These traits are believed to largely determine a person's behaviour, overriding the influence of the immediate social or cultural context or situation the person is involved in (Potter and Wetherell, 1987).

Personality tests such as those employed in some body image research rest on this notion of the self. Some body image researchers administered 'personality tests' to the subjects because, it was believed, the extent of body width over-estimation in anorexic subjects 'was significantly correlated with personality features' (Garner et al., 1976: 327). These features included the degree of neuroticism and low ego-strength, as measured on the Eysenck Personality Inventory. By correlating estimates of body width with a range of 'personality measures', researchers speculated on the causal relationship between psychological traits such as low self-esteem, depression and neuroticism, eating disorders and 'body image disturbance'. In body image disturbance studies (e.g. Garner et al., 1976, above) researchers linked their objective findings about personality traits to the test scores of women on body width estimation procedures. Researchers claim that if the scores on both tests, following statistical analysis, correlate positively, they form a 'picture' of a particular type of individual. Some researchers claim that anorexic women score highly on neuroticism trait scales and low on the trait of ego-strength, while overestimating their body width. These facts are interpreted as providing evidence of 'body image disturbance' as well as its cause, and comprise a profile of fixed, measurable psychological traits that classify a particular type of individual. Researchers look for relationships between 'psychological variables' they have identified, such as 'perfectionism, body dissatisfaction, asceticism, drive for thinness' and 'disordered eating' (see e.g. Ackard and Petersen, 2001).

Trait theory holds that personality traits form the individual as a comprehensive durable whole. Personality is at the centre of experience and initiates all action. The concept of each individual having a personality works to maintain a notion of 'the individual' as a separate bounded entity and assumes an individual–social dichotomy. Recent moves toward a contextual assessment of body image, with a greater emphasis on 'body image states' rather than 'traits', maintain the individual–social dichotomy (see e.g. Cash, 2002a), while some instruments produced to measure body image states, such as The Body Image States Scale, are 'appropriately correlated with various trait measures of body image' (Cash, Fleming, Alindogan, Steadman and Whitehead, 2002: 103).

Critics of trait theory argue against its asocial assumptions and assertions (e.g. Potter and Wetherell, 1987). Focusing on stable traits and patterns of behaviour is considered problematic because it ignores the variety and inconsistency of human behaviour.

Doing method – experimental procedures

Body image researchers, reflecting the methodological paradigm within which traditional psychology positions itself, assume that scientific methods of collecting data about women's estimations of body width and their 'beliefs and feelings' about their bodies (as objects) will guarantee progress towards complete knowledge of the condition they call 'body image disturbance'. This commitment to method as the route to truth is evidenced by the plethora of 'increasingly accurate' experimental measurement techniques researchers have invented. Developments over the past 25 years in body image research can be described almost entirely in terms of these inventions and the tenacity with which researchers have clung to method at the expense of theory, despite contradictory and inconclusive 'findings'.

Largely because they are so controllable, experimental conditions are considered most useful to developing consistent scientific knowledge. Good scientific knowledge is predicated on a researcher's ability to explain the reasons for events, behaviour and actions. In order to do this, it is considered most effective to manipulate at least one variable whilst holding others constant, within an experimental environment. Complex social processes need to be divided into identifiable and isolated (and therefore controllable) variables. Careful manipulation leads researchers to be able to 'reveal' cause-and-effect sequences of behaviour.

These causal sequences – the basis of psychological knowledge – are considered to express generalised laws of behaviour that have application outside the laboratory, in everyday life. In order to increase the likelihood of this universal

32

applicability, many experimental researchers claim to create in the laboratory the conditions of 'what would happen anyway' in everyday life. For example, in Slade and Russell's (1973: 190) studies of women's ability to estimate the width of their body parts, the subjects were wearing their normal clothes 'in order to provide the most natural situation for studying body image perception'.

The division of complex social phenomena into discrete controllable variables in the search for causal laws of behaviour is exemplified in Heinberg and Thompson's (1995) experiment. Heinberg and Thompson's interest was in 'the influence of a sociocultural factor on the development of body-image disturbance' (see also Thompson and Heinberg, 1999; Cusumano and Thompson, 2001). Within traditional psychological research it is believed that it is possible to operationalise and measure something called the 'sociocultural factor'. The authors had previously noted that: '. . . despite the acknowledgment of the importance of a sociocultural factor in the development and maintenance of body image disturbance, empirical research has been hindered by the lack of a measurement instrument designed to document such an influence' (Heinberg, Thompson and Stormer, 1995: 82).

In order to enable measurement, the researchers designed an experiment to 'expose women to societal images of thinness and attractiveness that are communi- cated through the televised media'. The 'sociocultural factor' was operationalised as 'viewing a 10-minute tape of advertisements that clearly communicated the current societal ideals of attractiveness'. The commercials featured women who represented societal ideals of thinness and attractiveness and included commercials for weight-loss supplements, automobiles, fast food and clothing. The control group watched a video 'devoid of such messages', featuring commercials for insurance policies and household cleaning products (Heinberg and Thompson, 1995: 328).

The experimental subjects were 138 'Caucasian female undergraduates', who were assigned to either an experimental group or a control group. The participants were given extra course credit for taking part in the experiment. The authors explained that one reason why the pool of subjects was narrowed to Caucasians was that the video materials consisted of commercials with primarily Caucasian characters. In this way, 'race' as a variable was screened out, and therefore is inevitably made insignificant – at least in this experiment – for thinking about how women view their bodies in a social context.

The participants were required to complete a series of psychological scales prior to viewing the video. These quantitative measures were the Sociocultural Attitudes Towards Appearance Questionnaire (SATAQ) and a scale measuring women's cognitive distortions related to physical appearance, the Bulimia Cognitive Distortions Scale–Physical Appearance Sub-scale (BCDS-PA). The researchers maintain that the SATAQ measures whether one is 'aware of societal pres- sures and/or "buys into" the messages (i.e. accepts and internalises these pressures, believing it is reasonable to strive to fit the societal stereotype)'. On the results of these tests, women were divided into two groups, identified as 'high and low levels of disturbance'. The third test administered was the Visual Analogue Scales (VAS), which measures immediate 'state' changes in body satisfaction and mood.

The VAS consisted of five measures: anxiety, depression, anger, body dis-satisfaction, and a 'VAS-overall appearance dissatisfaction'. The participants had to rate how they felt, from 'none' to 'very much', on each of these five dimensions, before and after the 'sociocultural influence' exposure (Heinberg and Thompson, 1995: 332–3).

After completing the measures, participants viewed the relevant videotape for their experimental condition in groups of two to eight in a small conference room. They were not given any particular rationale for the study but were told to watch 'as if you were watching television in your home', in order to make their responses as natural as possible. Following the video presentation, participants were required to complete the visual analogue scales. A statistical analysis led the researchers to the conclusion that 'media-presented images of thinness and attractiveness may negatively affect mood and body satisfaction' (Heinberg and Thompson, 1995: 332).

Interestingly, the researchers' particular assumptions about what counts as 'sociocultural factors' meant that they limited the subjects' social interactions in the laboratory. Sociocultural factors were considered to be only those dished up on the video screen, not those operating amongst the women (or between the subjects and researchers). Such supposed control over social variables ensures 'pure' data – and access to the truth about 'sociocultural effects'. As they put it: '. . . because there was no break between commercials presented via the videotape, participants were not given the opportunity to interact and contaminate each other's reactions to the manipulation' (Heinberg and Thompson, 1995: 332).

Their fear of contamination of 'pure' data reflects the researchers' belief that each woman can process the stimuli (television commercials) without interference, and this reflects their 'real' response. Ironically, a 'real' response to sociocultural factors is considered to occur independently of most of the social environment.

Researchers claim to reproduce the social context of women's lives via the 'controlled' viewing of television commercials. Here the sociocultural 'factor', that is the 'video-stimulus', is reduced to an independent variable, and separable from the person (the 'sociocultural' can be found and isolated, for example, in a 10-minute tape of television commercials). The formulation of this binary person/context has it that both elements are static rather than dynamically interrelated. It is assumed that a stable person with cognitive processes acts in a context that is fixed and separate, like a stage backcloth. The social context is seen as a possible influence on the individual, but both the individual and the societal 'influence' are conceptualised as two separate, self-contained, pre-constituted entities (Wetherell and Maybin, 1995). Language, the bearer of social meanings, has no place in the laboratory setting, where research tools have already predetermined what counts as meaning.

Another problematising assumption is the view of the individual – already formed in terms of characteristics or traits – as more or less consistent across different situations. The individual is reduced to an 'information-processing system' which can be mapped in terms of input and output. In this case, the perceptual input is the television commercials, and the output is the viewers' measurable responses on psychological scales. Researchers then infer the causal (cognitive) mechanisms that mediate between input and output. Heinberg and Thompson's (1995) explanation for the advertisements' negative effect on mood and body satisfaction is in terms of causal sequences of behaviour: '. . . perhaps the videotape primed appearance evaluative schemas, which led participants to compare themselves to the models portrayed in the advertisements, which led to negative feelings about their own body, which led to an overall dysphoric reaction' (Heinberg and Thompson, 1995: 335). The stimulus videotape activates cognitive structures which lead to (negative) feelings – with no reference to the social context.

The outcome of these investigative practices is a concept of 'body image disturbance' that locates the cause within the individual. The authors suggest that women most 'at risk' for a negative reaction to media messages are 'those who "buy into" societally presented images (as measured by the SATAQ)' (Heinberg and Thompson, 1995: 336). The solution to 'body image disturbance' is said to be found in the way in which some individuals 'cognitively challenge the messages communicated by the media' (Heinberg and Thompson, 1995: 327). For the researchers, the solution promises to take the form of normalising treatments for women: 'If clinical samples and/or persons with high levels of body image disturbance differ from relatively asymptomatic persons on schemas . . . and/or cognitive distortions, perhaps these individuals can be taught skills and strategies to lessen their distress when confronted with the omnipresent societal message that women must be attractive to be accepted' (Heinberg and Thompson, 1995: 337). These 'conclusions' both underline the notion of body image disturbance as a discrete and objectively categorisable cognitive problem, and also rely on the idea of body image 'problems' as individual pathology.

Work such as that of Heinberg and Thompson illustrates some of the key problems with experimental research. Complex social processes are reduced to controlled and measurable variables; highly artificial settings are believed to give access to the 'real' and the everyday; and causal explanations are said to be found in the discrete cognitive processes of individuals.

Statistical analysis

Further problems with experimental method relate to its reliance on statistical analysis for legitimate results. The use of *t*-tests and analyses of variance to draw conclusions from data is particularly common in the body image literature. Nearly every study described in the previous chapter had been subjected to a form of statistical analysis.

One potential difficulty for traditional psychology has been how to deal with variability that characterises complex human behaviour. In experimental studies, the behaviour of individual subjects may show little consistency from one occasion to another. The averaging of quantitative data from many subjects, or many studies, has been viewed as both a useful and acceptable way of handling this lack of consistency (Danziger, 1990). Influential research reviews often pool data from a range of studies in an attempt to report conclusive 'findings' from studies which may show diverse results (see e.g. Slade, 1985; Chapter 1). If data from many individuals is pooled, statistical regularities often emerge. These regularities form the basis of psychological generalisations, despite the fact that the average pattern may have little correspondence to the actual behaviour of any one of the individuals studied.

In body image research, this data 'analysis' has the effect of homogenising the sample of women to whom a study refers, concealing any individual variation within and between women. Averaged data and statistical analyses support psychology's claims to expert, consistent and exhaustive knowledge about women's views of their bodies. For instance, Thompson (1986) claims that 95% of the 100 white, middle-class, 'normal' women in his study over-estimate the size of their bodies. Subsequent reports of Thompson's research tend not to indicate sample size or composition, and imply that nearly all women over-estimate their body size (see e.g. Cash and Brown, 1987). Popular women's magazines do the same thing (see *Cleo* magazine, 1993, in Chapter 5).

References to 'females' ('women' is not a term used) in the body image literature inevitably imply one homogeneous group. The effect is to lose sight of crucial differences within and between women, and imply that we all have similar experiences. Differences of race, class, culture, ethnicity, sexual orientation, physical ability and the different 'histories' of women's lives and experiences are erased under the category 'female'.

Homogenisation is inevitable within the frame of experimental research. In its search for general laws of human behaviour, traditional experimental psychology seeks to provide an objective, explanatory account of a universal subject; someone not historically and socially situated. This account of the individual posits universally shared experience and understanding and universal patterns of behaviour. It is taken for granted that an authentic 'human nature' exists, which forms the basis of predictive formulations of human action (Gergen, 1994). Universalism functions to suppress variation, inconsistency and multiplicity, which are either ignored or suppressed via the scientific methods used to 'discover' universal truths.

The positivist research methods employed in body image research focus on quantifying women's bodies/subjectivities at the expense of their lived experience. This research literature posits psychological knowledge of women as both universal and representative, rather than the 'partial' account that it is. The following section takes a closer look at the controlled laboratory experiment and the ways in which it both rules out, and reproduces, gender, race, class and social/power relations. These relations, I argue, have a very significant effect on psychology's understanding of body image – and thus the understandings which have developed in the general population.

The body: the subject of the gaze

Body image researchers have defined the concept of body image as 'solely a physical appearance-related construct' (Thompson, 1990). This reproduces the common-sense view of women's bodies as an object of the gaze and reinforces the idea of women as observers of their own bodies. Current Western ideals of beauty and femininity rest on this notion: that physical appearance is constitutive of women's bodies/subjectivities. The intense interest in 'women's bodies' is focused on women's physical appearance (implicitly sexualised) and what women think and feel about the way they look. The emphasis on physical appearance reinforces the idea of women's bodies/subjectivities as primarily/essentially aesthetic. The idea that women's bodies are more than merely physical appearances, that they might be a product of social discourses, and experienced from 'within' or embodied, is precluded.

Although body image experiments are presented as neutral, objective scientific practices, these experiments do not occur in a social vacuum. They are a social practice which reproduces women's bodies/subjectivities within gendered power relations. The positioning of the women who are the object of these investigations *vis-à-vis* the researcher has particular effects for the knowledge that is produced. The body image experiment has at least two effects for the women subjects. By normalizing the practice of self-surveillance, experiments encourage women to view themselves as the objects of their own gaze. Second, the social context of the experiment reproduces gendered power relations via the masculine gaze of the experimenter/scientist.

Michel Foucault's (1990) concept of the Panopticon and disciplinary power remains the most insightful frame for arguing that body image investigations, rather than being simply an objective search for knowledge about women's bodies/subjectivities, are instead disciplinary and normalizing practices. Foucault points out that power is not primarily located externally to individuals or groups – that power relations come into being via the actions of individuals as they discipline themselves, in accordance with dominant norms and ideals. It is self-surveillance which 'assures the automatic functioning of power' (Foucault, 1990: 201).

So much, like during the day at work I think, 'Right, I've got to cover myself up, there can't be any breasts or bulges so I've got to have buttons, you know up to my neck more or less, or if not certainly decent so that no-one is distracted by anything. You know it's constantly an issue of 'how can I cover up and look noticeably smart but not noticeable in a funny sort of a way?'

Michel Foucault's analysis of power has been criticised for its lack of attention to the dimension of gender and the ways power operates differently on and through the bodies of men and women. Feminist writers such as Sandra Bartky have highlighted some of these differential effects, particularly the constant self-surveillance and the disciplinary practices in which Western women often engage in pursuit of the 'right' body size and shape. Bartky argues:

> The woman who checks her make-up half a dozen times a day to see if her foundation has caked or her mascara has run, who worries that the wind or the rain may spoil her hairdo, who looks frequently to see if her stockings have bagged at the ankle or who, feeling fat, monitors every-thing she eats, has become, just as surely as the inmate of the Panopticon, a self-policing subject, a self committed to a relentless self-surveillance. This self-surveillance is a form of obedience to patriarchy. It is also the reflection in the woman's consciousness of the fact that she is under surveillance in ways that he is not, that whatever else she may become, she is importantly a body designed to please or excite. There has been induced in many women, then, in Foucault's words, a 'state of conscious and permanent visibility that assures the automatic functioning of power'.
>
> (Bartky, 1988: 81)

There are parallels between the self-surveillance practised by many women in their daily lives and the self-surveillance re-enacted in the laboratory under the instruction and gaze of body image researchers. Both the researcher and the women subjects are to see her body as an object. They must scrutinise her body size and shape, and make 'accurate' and 'objective' estimations of the width of her face, chest, hips and thighs. Women must be able to make accurate estimations repeatedly over time and rationally appraise their body size and shape and 'get it right'.

These practices must be carried out under the gaze of the usually male researcher. It is in these practices legitimated as scientific research that the surveillance of women by men is normalised. (Male) researchers position themselves within a scientific discourse as arbiters of the truth about their subjects – in this case, women's bodies/subjectivities. Body image research normalises and reproduces those gendered social practices where men look at women's bodies/subjectivities and pass judgement on them.

Norris' (1984) study, outlined in detail in Chapter 1, provides an evocative example of gendered relations in an experimental context. In his study, '. . . the room lights were switched on and the subject, stripped semi-nude, was made to face a mirror . . . she was instructed to examine her body in stages from head to foot, noting her body size, running her fingers over the various fleshy and bony contours and outlining the four estimated diameters with her hands . . . throughout the entire experiment the tester adopted a completely neutral attitude . . . no reasons were given for the mirror confrontation and no comments were made about her body or any feelings she expressed' (Norris, 1984: 836–38). If we assume that the testers are male, we are left with an entirely distasteful image of a semi-nude woman 'running her fingers' over her body under the gaze of a silent man. Resonances with peep-shows and sexualised voyeurism cannot be avoided. While the same sexualised gaze may not always occur with a female tester, the sense of the always-scrutinised body as a (possibly imperfect) *object* is projected powerfully in the above account.

Seeing and being seen are never neutral activities, despite the 'neutral' researcher in the laboratory, looking at the woman's body. This issue – the effects of being looked at – is not raised by the experimental researchers. As Radley (1991) points out, 'an understanding of who sees, of how they see and of the significance of seeing in the social world is absent from psychological theory' (1991: 75). I would argue that the gaze in the body image experiment is *masculine*, not only because the researchers in this field are mostly male, but also because the idea of (women's) bodies as objects of perception, observed as it were from the 'outside', is an idea that derives from a 'masculine' point of view – necessarily 'outside' women, looking at them. Certainly women can and do learn to see their bodies as objects (take a masculine position, or take on a male gaze), but their experience of embodiment is necessarily more than this (something I discuss further). The gaze of psychology – in the sense of the theoretical 'spectacles' through which the subjects of psychology are 'seen' – is most certainly a male gaze (Gergen, 1996).

The significance of the male gaze to body image investigations is totally effaced. Claims to neutrality and value-free science extend to include the researcher as someone who exists outside of culture (including race and gender) and 'above the babble of politics' (Gergen, 1996). The claims of science to neutrality and to being value-free serve to mask the identity and the role of the 'expert' in constituting its object, in this case, women's bodies/subjectivities.

Feminist theorists (e.g. Gillian Rose, 1993) have argued that the form of rationality which underlies and forms science is masculine. Man is held to be the embodiment of reason, the one capable of rational thought in relation to the body of the Other (historically women, and Blacks, and working-class people), who is irrational, not capable of knowing. The researcher can come to know the Other/her through his neutral gaze. His ability to objectively perceive is not challenged, because (white) masculinity and neutrality are seen as synonymous.

It has been argued that masculine rationality is a form of knowledge which assumes a knower who believes that he is separate from his body, his emotions and values. He has no history. He and his thought are autonomous, objective and unitary. The assumption of an objectivity untainted by his social position(s) (as masculine, white, scientist) enables the knowledge produced via this kind of rationality to claim itself as universal and exhaustive. Both men and women scientists are trained to take the rational masculine position.

Within this discourse, men's bodies, represented by the body of the researcher, are produced as invisible. Because of his rational capacity for knowing, associated with the mind, the male/scientist is able to transcend the bodily aspect of his being.

If the researcher's gendered, classed and raced body is irrelevant to the knowledge formed in the experiment, the idea that knowledge is a product of social relations and cultural beliefs is automatically ruled out of consideration. These epistemic exclusions efface the ways in which psychology constitutes knowledge which is both historically and culturally specific. Of course, the researcher necessarily is embedded in wider social discourses and practices of gender. When the (male) researcher looks at the object of his research, he is positioned in relation to her, as both his identity and hers are already constructed through social relations of power.

Classification, normalisation, pathologisation

An interest in pathology characterises body image research (as well as much traditional psychology) and is evidenced in its very beginnings with the quest to locate a 'body image defect' (Fisher, 1986). Initially, investigations centred on groups of women with a diagnosis of anorexia nervosa, bulimia nervosa or obesity. The goal of these studies was objectively to measure differences in the way individual women perceived their body width in order to aid diagnosis of these eating disorders.

The testing of 'normal' women became necessary when researchers surmised that there were two groups of women – those who were able to estimate their 'real' body size, and those who could not. Those who could not were seen as disordered compared with 'normal' women, who could accurately estimate their body size. Women with an eating disorder were not capable of such a cognitive or perceptual feat. This disability (disturbance), and the anxiety (dissatisfaction) which accompanied it, defined their disorder. A network of researchers – psychologists, psychiatrists and doctors – defined what was normal, and what fell outside of that norm and was thus considered deviant. Early studies helped to reproduce and establish such categorisations. The rationale for investigating 'normal' women, and the process of classifying them as such, is intrinsic to comparative research methodologies which eventually provided researchers with access to, and justification for, measuring body width perception in all women (see e.g. Thompson, 1986).

J. Kevin Thompson's experimental investigations of 'normal' women, described in his own words in Chapter 1, were conducted on the basis that comparative studies of 'normal' women and those diagnosed with 'anorexia nervosa' sometimes showed that some 'normal' women over-estimated the width of their bodies, like their disordered peers. Thompson (1986) did not take this as evidence that 'body width perception' measures might not discriminate between women with eating disorders and those without, or that it might be an empty concept and no indicator of 'body image disturbance' or anything else. Instead, he and fellow researchers refocused their investigation of 'body image disturbance' to measure, test and classify 'normal' women.

What justified extending psychological surveillance to larger and larger groups of 'normal' women? The commitment of traditional experimental psychology to method at the expense of theory goes some way to explaining this. Once having discovered that 'body image disturbance' exists, researchers focused on improving its measurement and that of its causal relations (for instance, self-esteem). The narrow focus on method meant that it became unlikely that these researchers would ask questions about their underlying belief in the existence of the concept they were busy measuring.

It has been observed that medical regulation and intervention depend on representations of the body as fragile and remarkably subject to deviation from good health (Matus, 1995: 47). Within body image discourse, women are made objects of a discourse which constitutes them as irrational and unstable, with a weak body image and negative personality traits leading to pathology. This construction of 'women' allows for psychological intervention in the forms of a high level of external surveillance and involvement from science, medicine and psychology. The extension of psychological surveillance to 'normal' women brings into question the 'normality' of 'normal' women and destabilises that category.

When psychology turns its gaze on the 'normal' population, looking for pathology, it simultaneously implies that body image problems for most women are avoidable – that normal women can resist the spread of the problems of body image disturbance. That is, body image research lays blame for, and offers solutions to, the problem of 'body image disturbance' at the level of the (normal) individual. It holds that it is the responsibility of individual women to resist the pressures of society. Treatment programmes (e.g. Rosen, Saltzberg and Srebnik, 1989; see also Cash and Pruzinsky, 2002) that offer cognitive-behavioural therapy for individual women, in particular 'normal' women, underscore this assumption about the individual.

The search for pathology and the research methods employed in this endeavour together result in an intensification of women's bodies/subjectivities as objects of psychology's pathologising gaze. It constitutes women as isolated individuals who must resist societal influences and/or as in need of 'expert' psychological treatment.

If we assume that the goal of body image researchers was to understand the experiences of women who suffered from eating disorders and anxiety about their body size, what we have 25 years later is a discourse which potentially pathologises all women by creating a range of psychological classifications, including 'body image disturbance', 'body image dysfunction', 'body image distortion' and 'body image dissatisfaction'. Such labels have the effect of forming new subject positions or subjectivities (ways of understanding oneself) for all women (see next chapter). As Thompson puts it: 'it is apparent that serious clinically relevant body image dysfunction now exists in non-eating-disordered populations' (Thompson, 1990: 23).

The assumptions that form the basis of experimental body image research, including its mind–body dualism, perceptualism, realism and the society–individual dichotomy, are not the only ways of making sense of women's experiences of embodiment. In the following chapter I outline alternative formulations of women's embodiment and subjectivity. These approaches foreground language and meaning as forming women's experiences of their bodies, and I take these up in the final three chapters to illustrate a discursive approach to understanding or making sense of (some) women's difficult sense of embodiment – and the role of experimental body image research in constituting women's bodies/subjectivities.

3

DISCURSIVE CONSTITUTION OF
THE BODY

This chapter outlines a view of the body and subjectivity as discursive products –
a view in which all human experience is understood as cultural and social practice.
In such a perspective, in order to approach women's experiences of their bodies,
an analysis of the practices which constitute and regulate experience is required.
Experimental body image research, as we saw in the last two chapters, entirely
eschews such an approach in its assumptions that women's experience of their
bodies is simply perceptual and cognitive, and that women's difficult experiences
of their bodies are located in the minds of individual women.

In this chapter I set out a theoretical orientation for the empirical work in the
following three chapters. That work is an analysis of the discourses which inform
an important empirical site (popular women's magazines) of many women's
understandings of their bodies, and how these discourses are reproduced in one
woman's account of embodiment. I draw upon aspects of the diverse work of Susie
Orbach, Michel Foucault, Susan Bordo, Nikolas Rose, and Margaret Wetherell
and Jonathan Potter's discourse analytic work in social psychology, to provide
a theoretical framework within which to formulate an alternative understanding
of women's difficult experiences of their bodies.

A feminist constructionist view of the body and subjectivity

My interest in the theoretical contributions of Susie Orbach is in the very different
assumptions (from experimental psychology) that inform her understanding of
some women's fraught experiences of embodiment (see Orbach, 1978, 1986). Her
application of early feminist theory to this area of women's lives has powerfully
influenced the ways we can think about women's bodies/subjectivities.

Orbach, a British feminist psychotherapist, takes a social constructionist
view of the body and subjectivity. She foregrounds a social and political analysis
of women's experiences, stressing the primacy of meaning for understanding
subjectivity. Her work emerged from the 1970s feminist political movement,
with a popular audience and a commitment to a grounded social/political analysis.

Central to the development of this analysis was the process of consciousness-raising that enabled women to investigate, with other women, their experiences. Participants in these consciousness-raising groups shared the perspective that all women's experiences are a product of a patriarchal society which oppresses women. Discussions centred on women's experiences of their bodies, food, eating, dieting, thinness and fatness. The women recognised that all their attempts at 'getting our bodies the right weight and shape' had been unsuccessful. They questioned 'why we had wanted them so right?' and 'what was so powerful about looking a particular way that we had all tried and succeeded in losing weight dozens of times' (Orbach, 1988: 13–14).

For many women, this consciousness-raising process provided the possibility of challenging previously held assumptions that difficulties and problems they experienced (e.g. feeling anxious about their body size/shape) were due to personal failure or inadequacy. Orbach suggested that there were good reasons why women develop problems with food, eating and their bodies. She argued that it had nothing to do with will-power, or lack of it, and everything to do with women's subordinate social position *vis-à-vis* men in patriarchal society. Women were socialized to conform to a particular body shape in order to be sexually attractive to, and compete for, a man who would then, supposedly, take care of her economic needs.

This argument signalled a radical departure from the dominant discourse which positioned women as responsible for their own 'obsession' with dieting, body size/shape and physical appearance (and also marked a shift to women-as-victims of patriarchy). Blaming women for their preoccupation with appearance drew on historical constructions of women as 'narcissistic' and 'naturally' interested and involved in the daily routines of food restriction, anxiety about body weight and preoccupation with physical appearance.

The struggles of early feminists were encapsulated in the concept of 'body as battleground'. Women's rights to abortion, anti-rape campaigns and opposition to compulsory heterosexuality centred on a woman's right to control her body. Women's bodies were seen as a site of contestation, as a focal point for the struggles of power. This early feminist model reconceptualised the body from simply a biological form to a historical construction and a medium of social control.

Orbach's work was important to the establishment of the body as a legitimate area for political concern. She and others used this political view of women's bodies to inform their understanding of women's sexuality, beauty and 'femininity'. They challenged the 'naturalness' of these discourses, embedding them in a social/political context. Dominant norms of femininity were seen as socially constructed and oppressive to women (Orbach, 1988: 24).

Orbach distinguished between the biological or the 'natural' body and the ways that the body is represented and given meaning. She argued that it is the way that women and women's bodies are represented that results in the oppression of women. Orbach maintained a distinction between the mind and the body, which she reinterpreted as a distinction between sex and gender.

Language in Orbach's formulation is 'a complex of social and personal meanings' which women express through their talk about their bodies and food. A woman may use the word 'fat' to convey how she feels about her body, irrespective of body size, '. . . so when I speak of "fat" or "thin" . . . I am exploring what seeing herself in this way means for her'. Orbach stressed the importance of recognising the extent to which the words 'fat', 'thin' and 'overweight' are not just physically descriptive, '. . . they carry social meaning, fantasies, projections . . . ' (Orbach, 1988: 2–3).

I'd always believed you became transformed once you were thin. Everything in your life works out, everything. You are attractive and fun to be with. I got thin and it never happened. Being thin was uncomfortable because I am short and got really thin. I hated it because I felt little. I was very conscious of my size, that physically I looked small and tiny, but I don't feel like that inside. You're trying to look like a mannequin, like a model, but you actually have a personality in there and it doesn't necessarily fit the body.

This view radically contrasts with that of experimental psychologists who argue that a woman claiming to be fat whilst emaciated was not seeing her body 'as it really was', and that 'normal' women 'got it wrong' when they 'over-estimated' or 'under-estimated' their body size. Experimental psychologists' view that women's body image is more or less stable over time is undercut by Orbach's recognition of women's experiences as having multiple meanings and interpretations: 'fat' or 'thin' will mean different things for different women at different times. At the same time, she makes clear the impact of cultural representations of femininity on 'how we wish to represent ourselves', stressing how our own ideas about ourselves are inextricable from those representations (Orbach, 1988: 24).

For Orbach, then, the origin or cause of women's difficult experiences of their bodies lies not in the minds of individual women, but in the inequality of the sexes. This social inequality, she says, based on 'innate differences', has become institutionalised in the unequal gendered division of labour. Women's relegation to the social roles of wife and mother, Orbach argues, contributes to the difficulties women have around food and their bodies because 'getting a man' is held out as a crucial goal for women. 'To get a man, a woman must learn to regard herself as an item, a commodity, a sex object. Much of her experience and identity depends on how she and others see her' (Orbach, 1988: 22). Orbach argues that this representation of women defines them in a particular relationship to men and to themselves; 'Men act and women appear. Men look at women, women watch themselves being looked at. This determines not only most relations between men and women, but also the relationship of women to themselves' (Berger, 1972: 47; cited in Orbach, 1988: 29–30).

I'm becoming more comfortable with being a mother than with the idea of being a woman who is sexually attractive. It's hard to be both, it's like you're meant to be either one or the other. Then you look at the magazines that say 'you can be a mother and be beautiful', separating all those nice-looking women who have managed to regain their figure and have careers and be fantastic mothers as well, it is separating them into another group and that bugs me. It is fantastic for them but it makes it worse for all the ordinary women, all the women that are overweight. It is setting up a standard that I feel if I can't achieve that there is something wrong with me I guess. It is achievable for them and I am just as good as they are so why can't I achieve it? I guess I don't want to go through life and then everyone remember me as this lovely cuddly mum or this overweight person.

This relationship of 'women to themselves' emphasises self-presentation as the central aspect of a woman's existence. A woman is required to develop or fashion a self-image that others will find attractive. She must 'observe and evaluate herself, scrutinizing every detail of herself as though she were an outside judge. She attempts to make herself in the image of womanhood presented by billboards, newspapers, magazines and television' (Orbach, 1988: 30). For Orbach, this preoccupation with appearance and 'self-image' encourages many, if not most, women to view themselves 'from the outside' as candidates for men. This means that women can become prey to the fashion and diet industries, which promote the ideal images of femininity and then exhort women to meet them.

Western standards demand that a woman's body be 'thin, free of "unwanted hair", deodorized, perfumed and clothed. It must conform to an ideal physical type' (Orbach, 1988: 30–31). Socialisation within the family and at school trains girls to 'groom' themselves appropriately. Orbach points out that this work is never-ending. The models of femininity are constantly changing, extolling 'new' images of proper womanhood.

Because few women's bodies fit the ideal, most women 'must' fail to measure up to current standards of femininity. But to ignore them is to risk being an outcast, from femininity, desirability and normality. Orbach claims that women experience the 'ideal' images as unattainable, frightening and unrealistic. This means that women's bodies are always in danger of not being 'their own'; they are not satisfactory as they are (Orbach, 1988, 1999).

For Orbach, any 'solutions' to the difficulties many women have with food, bodies and eating require changes in existing social conditions (Orbach, 1986). As well, she argues (talking here about women with anorexia nervosa, but it is a theme which pervades all of her work), it is necessary for a woman not to regard her body as an object to be moulded and shaped but instead to develop 'the ability to experience the body as the place one lives in . . . she has to find a way of reconciling the body as owned and lived in with the opposing cultural thrust of the female body as object' (Orbach, 1986: 153).

The particular feminist theoretical framework in which Orbach's work is located has been critiqued more recently by a range of feminist philosophers and theorists (e.g. Bordo, 1993a, 1993b; Butler, 1990; Grosz, 1994; McNay, 1992). However, I would argue that features of Orbach's work can provide useful insights into difficulties women continue to experience with eating and body size today. What I want to take forward from Orbach's work for the analyses in the following chapters is an emphasis on the political and gendered nature of women's experiences; the inseparability of 'the personal' from 'the political'. Here, the political includes both 'big electoral and governance-based politics' as well as the 'little politics' of everyday life, derived from the organization of social relations and the ways in which these are infused with power.

Especially important is the notion that the individual does not exist in a social vacuum, that subjectivity (including our experience of and understanding of our bodies) is constituted through discourses that are socially and historically specific. Although Orbach did not use this language (which developed in the late 1980s), she identified discourses of 'femininity' which converge upon the female body and continue to constitute and regulate our experiences of embodiment, gender and subjectivity in early twenty-first century Western society.

Second, Orbach's emphasis on language and the importance of meaning was a precursor to later developments in feminist work. Orbach saw the female body as invested with meanings that are both multiple and contradictory. Her analysis allowed for a multiplicity of meanings (or 'truths') and for an understanding of subjectivity as both inconsistent and contradictory, rather than unitary and rational.

Third, in viewing the body as socially produced, not simply a biological object, early feminists such as Orbach understood it as a medium for power and social control, a site of struggle and contestation.

Orbach's work is also useful as it draws attention to cultural assumptions reproduced in women's and men's everyday talk about women's bodies, femininity, beauty and sexuality. One of the main weaknesses of Orbach's position is her implicit theory of power. This notion of power as always-already repressive has been critiqued more recently by feminist theorists employing a Foucauldian analysis of power.

Foucault and the socially produced body

Drawing on the work of French philosopher/historian Michel Foucault, feminist theorists have developed ideas about the relationship between the body and power which provide a different formulation from that within which Orbach worked (e.g. Butler, 1990; McNay, 1992). In Orbach's analysis, women appear as largely victims of patriarchal desires, rather than as social actors who might *participate* in predominant social practices and ideologies. Power, from the sort of view informing Orbach's and other radical feminists' work, is understood as something that 'belongs' to one group and is wielded over others who do not 'have' it. In patriarchal society, this means that the oppressors (men) 'have' power and exercise it over the oppressed (women).

Other feminists have argued that women can be understood – and should be understood – not simply as passive victims but as active agents, actively and knowingly engaging in practices that could be understood as oppressive (e.g. Bordo, 1993a).

Such a perspective is underpinned by a view of power espoused by Foucault, which does not position women and other 'oppressed groups' outside of power, as powerless. Rather, power is exercised by all (except those physically restrained) and the strength of power is precisely in this fact. People engage (with power) in active self-discipline, (usually) living out dominant social ideas – which is why they are 'dominant'. Power is not a matter of top-down coercion but a productive force, because power creates knowledge:

> Power produces knowledge (and not simply by encouraging it because it serves power or by applying it because it is useful); . . . power and knowledge directly imply one another . . . there is no power relation without the correlative constitution of a field of knowledge, nor any knowledge that does not presuppose and constitute at the same time power relations.
>
> (Foucault 1977: 27)

Take, for example, the power relations which constitute knowledge claims about 'body image' discourse. Not only is this knowledge mostly created by white, male scientists and their particular views of the world, but it has material effects that produce a particular body/subjectivity – that is, women with 'body image disturbance' or women and girls as vulnerable to developing 'body image disturbance'. The practices that make up that field of knowledge can be seen to regulate the behaviour of many women because these practices constitute 'reality' in particular ways.

The work of Foucault has been extensively drawn on by feminist theorists to provide a broader philosophical grounding for understanding not only power, but also the role of language in the production of subjectivity. According to Foucault, power 'works' via language, which forms and is formed by social organisation. Subjectivity (or sense of self) is constructed in language (and thus within the cultural and social order). In this view subjectivity is not the reflection of an innate or essential individual consciousness (the 'individual' at the centre of body image investigations), but is theorised as being constructed through language in ways that are socially specific. Subjectivity is not fixed or unitary but, like the social order through which it is produced, is a site of movement, disunity, conflict and contestation.

For Foucault, language or, in its broadest sense, discourse is central. It 'transmits and produces power' (Foucault, 1990: 101). Language, in Foucault's view, is not unitary and trans-historical but instead consists of a range of different socio-historical discourses, such as economic, legal and psychological discourses. Foucault uses 'discourse' to refer to groups of statements which cohere around a particular topic or object, providing a way of talking about that topic (as with body image discourse). These statements can be produced across a range of different texts or institutional sites but are connected by an underlying regularity.

Discourses are social practices 'that systematically form the objects of which they speak' (Foucault, 1972: 49). That is, discourse is constitutive of subjectivity, objects, events and experience. Discourses offer multiple, competing, and potentially contradictory ways of giving meaning to the world.

Concepts or categories such as 'woman' and 'femininity' are multiply produced across a range of discourses that simultaneously constitute and regulate the female body, in often contradictory ways (Grosz, 1994; Malson, 1998; Ussher, 1997a).

Discourses produce subject positions or 'identities' from which a person can speak or be addressed. A Foucauldian perspective thus reconceptualises the 'individual' of traditional psychology in radical ways. The individual is replaced by multiple subject positions constituted in discourse. Instead of reflecting the essential, unitary and unique nature of an individual (e.g. as in psychology's trait theory of personality), discourses produce a range of possible subject positions which people live out/through (see Henriques et al., 1984; Weedon, 1987).

Discourses differ in their authority. Dominant discourses appear as commonsense or 'natural' and support and reproduce existing power relations (see e.g. the discourse of self-improvement predicated on the assumptions that women's bodies are flawed and in need of remedial work; Chapter 4). Dominant systems of meaning, such as femininity equals slenderness and docility, tend to constitute the subjectivity of (most) people most often in any given socio-historical context. Other, less dominant or marginalised discourses (e.g. feminist discourses) are not as available as subject positions through which women may meaningfully act and understand themselves and others.

The body produced by power

In Foucault's work, and implied differently in the work of Orbach and the early feminists, the body is produced by power. Foucault's concept of the body goes beyond that of the early feminists. In Orbach's work, the body is conceptualised as the 'natural' body overlaid with the social. On a Foucauldian view, the body is thoroughly social, produced within power/discourse. In contrast to the dominant Cartesian view of the body as simply housing a privileged consciousness, Foucault conceives the body as a concrete form which is the focus of the material forces of power relations. In this formulation, the body is the locus of practical cultural control. Discursive/social practices that work on and through the body have material effects that produce us as subjects (Foucault, 1990).

I was 52 years old and out of shape. I had 33% of fat in my back alone and I went down to 15%. And I was 69.8 kilos and I went down to 56 kilos, within 12 weeks, and I lost all the flab under my arms. I was doing a 70-hour week at work plus an hour of weight training in the morning and an hour of cardio at night. So I did 2 hours at the gym every day, 7 days a week. I didn't have to do that but the more disciplined I am the better I focus.

Through daily practices, bodies become 'docile' bodies subject to external regulation, to modes of transformation, self-surveillance and improvement. 'Modern power' both produces and normalises bodies in ways that serve current social relations of dominance and subordination. Power is heterogeneous and dispersed in nature, 'regulating the most intimate and minute elements of the construction of space, time, desire and embodiment' (Foucault, 1990: 138).

For Foucault the body is both 'object and target of power'. He described the body as being 'in the grip of very strict powers, which imposed on it constraints, prohibitions or obligations'. The effects of power on the body function by 'exercising upon it a subtle coercion, of obtaining holds upon it at the level of the mechanism itself – movements, gestures, attitudes, rapidity: an infinitesimal power over the active body' (Foucault, 1990: 136–7). The idea that power relations and technologies of power operate on human bodies, inscribing them in particular ways, is evident in body image research, where psychometric 'personality' tests mark women's bodies as neurotic and unstable (and so on) and experimental procedures mark women's bodies as pathological.

Usefully, for those of us interested in the body, Foucault was most interested in power in terms of its 'micro-physics' – the many localized circuits, tactics, mechanisms and effects through which power operates. For Foucault the body is the site on which the 'micro-physics' of power works – the site of discursive struggles between different power/knowledge regimes. The body is inscribed and classified according to different formations of power/knowledge and different regimes of power. This means the body is produced within discourse according to the discursive formations in circulation at any particular socio-historical moment (Foucault, 1977).

Weight Watchers the second time around was just horrific. I got really upset going back, it totally threw me, all week I was just an absolute wreck and food was right there in front of my face. You are given this book and you're supposed to eat one apple here and half a cup of this and 3 ounces of that and I just can't, it's totally not me. The instructor who was standing up the front of the dais said, 'Well girls, I've been a member of Weight Watchers

> for 20 years and I'm still coming along. I'm on a maintenance programme',
> and I looked and thought, 'Oh God, there's no way I want to be coming
> along here for 20 years'.

A range of discourses, of femininity, sexuality, self-improvement, self-acceptance, as well as body image discourse, to name a few, converge on the female body in contemporary Western society. These discursive formations position women in often contradictory ways. For instance, a discourse of self-improvement centred on women's physical appearance constitutes women's bodies/subjectivities as needing remedial work. At the same time, a discourse of self-acceptance (evident in body image discourse) positions women as 'pathological' if they do not accept their bodies as they are (see Chapters 4 and 5).

Body image discourse is only one of a range of systems of meaning, representation and power relations in which women's bodies are enmeshed. However the notion of 'body image' and the explanation of 'body image dissatisfaction/disturbance' is becoming one of the central discursive resources currently available to women and girls for making sense of their complex experiences of their bodies. Body image discourse/knowledge now mediates many women's self-understandings, actively constructing the cultural meanings we give to food, eating and body size/shape. Other interpretations or meanings of women's difficult experiences around food and body size are suppressed. Body image discourse defines what can be said and thought about (many) women's difficult experiences with food, eating and wanting to change the size and shape of their bodies. 'Body image' is given the status of a psychological object, which renders it 'real'; it can be named and described (Foucault, 1972).

> 'SPECIAL: Build a Better Body Image. Feel Good Naked. Would you
> rather die than take off your clothes? Read Laurie Redmond, who cured
> herself of body hatred with a ten-point program that can bring any woman
> to her senses'. *O – The Oprah Magazine*, October 2001.

Foucault was not concerned with whether a particular knowledge was 'true' but with the 'truth-effects of power', the question of when and where power/knowledge is applied and the 'effectivity' of this application, that is, the effects of that knowledge. He argued there are certain types of discourse in each society that are accepted and allowed to function as the 'truth' (e.g. scientific discourses such as body image discourse):

> Truth isn't outside power or lacking in power . . . Truth is a thing of this
> world; it is produced only by virtue of multiple forms of constraint. And

it induces regular effects of power. Each society has its regime of truth, its 'general politics' of truth; that is, the types of discourse which it accepts and makes function as true: the mechanisms and instances which enable one to distinguish true and false statements, the means by which each is sanctioned . . . the status of those who are charged with saying what counts as true.

(Foucault, 1980: 131)

Subjectification

Individuals are subjected to, or become subjects of, particular discursive formations through the operation of power within discourse. Power/discourse subjects individuals by prescribing and shaping human behaviour and action according to specific norms. Norms function to delimit individuals in particular ways but they also enable certain forms of agency. Foucault stressed in his later work that modern power relations are never seamless. Instead, power relations are constantly producing new forms of culture and new forms of subjectivity, and thus new possibilities of resistance (Foucault, 1990).

Foucault, in his later works, modified his understanding of how power relations form the actions of individuals. Foucault's emphasis on the overarching effects of power, in his early writings, resulted in a monolithic and functional account of power (McNay, 1992). The effects of power upon the body led to an account of human beings as passive or docile bodies. Foucault's early account weighted an analysis of techniques of domination at the expense of an understanding of techniques of the self (Foucault, 1985; see also McNay, 1992). Techniques or practices of the self refer to the process whereby an individual comes to understand him/herself as a subject. A focus on techniques and practices of the self centred on a more dynamic understanding of the ways in which individuals make sense of their experiences, as:

> . . . the games of truth and error through which being is historically constituted as experience; that is, as something that can and must be thought. What are the games of truth by which man proposed to think his own nature when he perceives himself to be mad; when he considers himself to be ill; when he conceives of himself as a living, speaking, labouring being?

(Foucault, 1985: 6–7)

According to this argument, human beings actively shape their own existence by adopting various discursive/social practices, rather than their behaviour being merely a reflection of 'overarching ideologies and systems of belief' (McNay, 1992: 59). The shift in emphasis from body to self enabled Foucault to attribute a degree of autonomy and independence to the actions of individuals. But Foucault emphasised that his idea of the self was not that of the sovereign individual:

52

> I believe that there is no sovereign, founding subject, a universal form
> of subject to be found everywhere. I am very sceptical of this view of
> the subject . . . I believe, on the contrary, that the subject is constituted
> through practices of subjection, or, in a more autonomous way, through
> practices of liberation.
>
> (Foucault 1985: 50)

In saying that the subject constitutes him/herself in an active fashion, Foucault
does not mean that the individual invents these practices. Rather, these practices
are 'patterns that he finds in his culture and which are proposed, suggested
and imposed on him by his culture, his society and his social group' (Foucault,
1988: 11).

The socially produced body is inscribed through a process of subjectification,
where subjects become subjects through the discourse that they speak. Subjects
'speak themselves into being', using the patterns available in culture. This form
of inscription is dependent on the concept of normalization. For Foucault, 'normalization is at the core of all techniques, practices, knowledges and discourses'
(Dreyfus and Rabinow, 1982). The idea of the 'norm' is at the heart of surveillance, establishing what is 'normal' and classifying people in relation to this norm.
Norms serve as models against which the self continually judges, measures,
disciplines and corrects itself.

I had lots of strict dieting regimes at school. I went through this stage when
I was nursing, of discovering how to be bulimic, though it didn't have
that term then. So many of us were doing it, it seemed normal I guess but
nobody had really put a name to it. I got really solidly into doing that. The
only pleasure in my life at that time was eating and I didn't want the
consequences of eating. I tried the gym, that Slender You thing and got some
pills in high school. I was on Ponderax from the doctor for years and years.
They're an appetite suppressant. I don't think it was an amphetamine or
anything but I know I felt funny when I tried to stop taking them.

Elizabeth Grosz and other feminists have criticised Foucault for his tendency to
assume a normatively male body when speaking of the body and for omitting
to take into account the different effects power/discourse produces on/through
the bodies of men and women (Butler, 1990; Grosz, 1994; McNay, 1992).
Notwithstanding this, Foucault's work has been taken up and utilised, in different
ways, within a range of feminist projects (see e.g. Bartky, 1988; Butler, 1990;
Gavey, 1992; Grosz, 1994; Sawicki, 1991).

Foucault's theory of the body as a socio-historical specificity has been crucial
for many feminists. The body has traditionally been viewed as a natural entity
rather than a historically and socially specific cultural product. On the basis of

biological differences between male and female bodies, women's inferiority to men has been naturalised and deemed legitimate.

Historically, women's bodies have been constituted as lack in relation to men's bodies. The material effects of negative misogynist representations of women's bodies in constituting and regulating women's bodies have been well documented (e.g. Showalter, 1987; Ussher, 1989, 1991). To view the body not as natural, fixed, ahistorical and asocial but as socially produced and always, already constituted through discourse (McNay, 1992), opens up the possibility of action and positivity rather than passivity and oppression (see e.g. Grosz, 1994). Understanding the body as socially produced demands an analysis of the ways in which women's bodies have been constituted (in this case through the scientific discourse of experimental psychology's body image research) as pathology.

Of significance for my analysis of body image discourse is the reliance of body image research on the concept of a 'natural' body that exists outside the social and meaning. A view of the body as socially produced highlights the impossibility of seeing one's body 'as it really is' and accepting one's body 'as it really is'.

Normalisation and self-discipline

Feminist philosopher Susan Bordo examines how power produces women's bodies through practices of 'body management', which encompass the restriction of food intake and excessive exercising in pursuit of an 'ideal' physical body size and shape (Bordo, 1993a, 1993b). Bordo's feminist politics of the body, centred on the politics of appearance, is a cultural critique informed by Foucault's writings on modern power, normalisation and surveillance.

Bordo's feminist cultural critique, centred on the reproduction of femininity, is useful for my analysis of how women's bodies are produced through experimental psychology's body image discourse in different empirical sites. Cultural practices that produce women's bodies are also the focus of Bordo's analysis. She emphasises the primacy of practice over belief in understanding and analysing the normalizing role of cultural practices. Bordo provides a way of understanding how women come to regulate and discipline their own bodies in relation to dominant social norms of femininity (Bordo, 1993a, 1993b).

I am pretty sure that lots of people, until they get to know me, judge me as being a large woman, a larger woman who has probably got children and just lives a house-wifey kind of life. People probably don't see my sense of humour as much and I am not as confident especially around men because I feel that I am less attractive than other women.

The notion of modern power, in Foucault's writings, is central to Bordo's critique of cultural practices that reproduce femininity. An understanding of how power operates means conceptualising power as exercised rather than possessed, productive, not primarily repressive, and an analysis of dominance as achieved not from above but from the bottom up, through a range of heterogeneous processes and practices of varied origin and scattered location (Bordo, 1993b). Non-authoritarian and non-conspiratorial, modern power produces and normalises bodies in ways 'that serve relations of dominance and subordination, so much of which is reproduced 'voluntarily' through self-normalisation to everyday habits of masculinity and femininity' (Bordo, 1993b: 190). For example, gendered social and cultural discourses of eating and appetite and representations of idealized bodies inform and produce a range of self-regulatory practices (see also Hepworth, 1999; Robertson, 1992). These self-regulatory practices become a form of discipline of the body. Such practices include the ways in which many women continually struggle with food in order to regulate their appetite and body weight.

> Almost every woman has had some experience of dieting. Watching what she eats becomes second nature, just a part of being a woman. Women make many different adaptations to the strictures against eating. There are those women who are constantly dieting and consistently limiting their food intakes; there are those women who diet during the week and 'let themselves go' at weekends; there are those women who don't eat until suppertime; there are those women who substitute liquid protein for meals several times a week; there are those women who fast once a week; there are those women who haven't eaten potatoes, butter or dessert in years; there are those women who go to health clubs to work off their 'indulgences'; there are those women who binge and then vomit (bulimics); there are those women who consistently plan to diet but end up overeating every time they start to eat something (compulsive eaters); there are those women who try to avoid food at all costs (anorectics).
>
> (Orbach, 1986: 61).

Dominant forms of subjectivity (or identity) are maintained, not through physical restraint or coercion, but through self-surveillance and self-correction to social norms.

My analysis does not centre simply on the reproduction of gendered power relations within the practices which surround 'body image'. I focus specifically on practices of self-surveillance and self-normalisation, through a closer reading of texts (i.e. talk about 'body image' in popular women's magazine and one woman's account) which produce women's bodies.

Normalisation, says Bordo, can be understood as the 'modes of acculturation' which function by setting up standards (or norms) against which individuals measure, judge, discipline and 'correct' their behaviour and appearance. Normalisation – central to notions of body image – is central to the workings of power (Bordo, 1993b: 199). Normalisation offers a way of understanding how women come to regulate their own behaviour in particular – often oppressive – ways. It can 'work' via such subtle means as 'a gaze':

> There is no need for arms, physical violence, material constraints. Just a gaze. An inspecting gaze, a gaze which each individual under its weight will end by interiorising to the point that he is his own overseer, each individual thus exercising his surveillance over and against himself.
>
> (Foucault, 1977: 155)

The body, in Bordo's work, is a practical direct locus of social control. A preoccupation with fat, diet and slenderness (affecting mainly women) may function, she says, as 'one of the most powerful normalizing strategies of our century, ensuring the production of self-monitoring and self-disciplining 'docile bodies' sensitive to any departure from social norms, and habituated to self-improvement and transformation in the service of these norms' (Bordo, 1993a: 186).

Resistance and victimisation

Bordo argues that there are at least 'two Foucaults' for feminism. The first is characterised by an understanding of the systemic grip of power on the body and emphasises the production of self-disciplining 'docile bodies' (see Bartky, Chapter 2, and also Bartky, 1988, for an example of this interpretation of Foucault). A second reading of Foucault emphasises the creative power of bodies to *resist* that grip (e.g. Haraway, 1991).

In her own work Bordo acknowledges that both perspectives are crucial to a theoretical understanding of the workings of power through the body. She argues that emphasising the grip of power on the body through normalising and disciplinary practices, rather than emphasising creative resistance, is more fruitful for an understanding of the specific historical situations of women in contemporary Western society. She emphasises the grip of power on the body because of the prevailing relation of women's bodies to 'the image industry' of post-industrial capitalism, a context, Bordo argues, in which anxiety about body weight and eating disorders proliferates. An effect of the relationship between women's bodies and the image industry is that women's physical appearance is increasingly understood as malleable, able to be changed, as we choose, at will.

I share Bordo's emphasis on the normalising power of dominant social . standards of beauty and femininity, because it underscores the power of norms of physical appearance to shape and move the body. In experimental body image research, norms of beauty are relegated simply to external 'sociocultural factors'. Within the empirical site of popular women's magazines (the context of my analyses of body image discourse in Chapters 4 and 5), these standards powerfully shape and define women's desires, experiences and bodies, including 'teaching' women how to see their bodies in comparison with that norm (Bordo, 1993a). Bordo's argument is important for my work because she provides a critical feminist analysis that emphasises the power of normalising imagery and dominant discourses of femininity, within which experimental psychology's body image discourse is embedded in popular women's magazines.

IT IS FAR BETTER TO BE LOOKED OVER THAN IT IS TO BE OVERLOOKED (Advertising slogan, young women's fashion store).

Finally, a key element in Foucault's concept of power that informs Bordo's work, and is important for mine, is the way that normative feminine practices (including dieting and other body management techniques) 'train the female body in docility and obedience to cultural demands, while simultaneously these practices are often experienced in terms of 'power' and 'control' (Bordo, 1993b: 192). Bordo argues that feeling powerful or 'in control' 'is not necessarily an accurate reflection of one's social position, is always suspect as itself the product of power relations whose shape may be very different' (Bordo, 1993b: 192).

In her work, Bordo emphasises the importance of normalisation and self-surveillance to an understanding of how women's bodies are produced (as femininity). She points out that disciplinary practices can be experienced in terms of power and control, seemingly liberatory rather than disciplinary and self-regulating. Bordo grounds her work in the contemporary cultural practices that produce women's bodies in particular ways.

Practices of subjectification

The practices within which people are addressed and located are also a focus of British sociologist Nikolas Rose's history of 'the contemporary regime of the self'. Rose has also derived a great deal from Foucault's writings and his work provides a conceptual bridge into my empirical research, from the broader framework of Foucault's own writings.

Rose's history of the self is an analysis of how heterogeneous practices produce human beings as persons of a certain kind. There are three aspects of Rose's work I want to outline here. First, the constitutive role of psychology in practices of subjectification, that is, the role of psychology in making up the kinds of people we take ourselves to be. For Rose, our contemporary regime of the self is a regulative ideal and a historical invention. Rose argues that the 'psy disciplines', that is, psychology, psychiatry and psychotherapy, in their very different forms, have all played a role in constituting our current regime of the self. Psychology, in his view (and to a lesser extent psychoanalysis and psychotherapy), has penetrated contemporary Western culture and 'played a rather fundamental part in "making up" the kinds of persons that we take ourselves to be' (Rose, 1996: 10). In this view, psychology is not a set of abstracted ideas and explanations but an 'intellectual technology', '. . . a way of making visible and intelligible certain features of persons, their conducts, and their relations with one another' (Rose 1996: 10–11). Psychology, in Rose's view, is not a purely academic activity but is better understood as an enterprise grounded in a relation between psychology's place in the academy and its place as expertise (Rose, 1996; see also Danziger, 1990).

From Rose's perspective, the history of the 'psy disciplines' is also a history of the ways in which human beings have regulated their own actions and those of others in terms of, to use Foucault's term, certain 'games of truth' (Rose, 1996). The history of 'psy' is intrinsically tied to a history of government. Rose uses the term 'government' in the much broader sense accorded it by Foucault. For Rose, the term 'government' is a useful way of conceptualizing the 'more or less rationalized programs, strategies, and tactics for the "conduct of conduct", for acting upon the actions of others in order to achieve certain ends' (Rose, 1996: 12; see also Rose, 1990). For Rose, psychology supplies the vocabularies and narratives by which we come to understand ourselves. Experimental psychology's body image research practices (see Chapter 1) and psychological strategies for improving body image problems (see Chapter 5) exemplify tactics for acting upon the actions of others in order to achieve certain ends – knowledge about body image in the first example and changing women's conduct in the latter.

Second, our contemporary concept of the self is understood in terms of autonomy, identity, individuality, liberty, choice and fulfilment. Rose argues that it is in these terms that we understand our desires and passions, shape our lifestyles, consume particular commodities, fashion and display our bodies and so on. This notion of the free, autonomous self is fundamental to the relationship of our self to our self, that is, the ways in which we come to understand, experience and judge our everyday lives. This notion of the self is implicitly a natural, a given, not an aim or a norm. For Rose, this regulative ideal of the self both capacitates and governs us in different ways in different practices and sites.

The regulative ideal of the autonomous, freely choosing self means that human beings are addressed, within a range of heterogeneous practices, as subjects of a certain kind – 'coherent, bounded, intentional, the locus of thought, action and belief . . . possessing an identity, which constitutes our deepest, most profound reality' (Rose, 1996: 3–4). Common-sense understandings hold that, as 'selves', we are individuals 'inhabited by an inner psychology that animates and explains our conduct and strives for self-realization, self-esteem and self-fulfilment in everyday life' (Rose, 1996: 3). Psychology (and other 'psy' disciplines) has mediated the techniques and practices of everyday life through a language which transforms notions of freedom into subjective, psychological states. Psychology mediates practices offering the possibility of fulfilment and self-actualisation through a relationship with the self. This works through the idea of what is normal. We have come to accept that it is normal to strive for and achieve a state of personal or individual freedom in our lives. Our lives, Rose argues, are made meaningful by the extent to which 'we can discover our self, be our self, express our self, love our self and be loved for the self we really are' (Rose, 1996: 4).

> I tell you, by the time I had lost all that weight I felt such a sexy lady I thought, 'Listen, I can do anything now'. But you see, it took feeling confident about my body for me to feel feminine again, and I had to do something because the way I looked at it was, I am nearly fifty and if I don't do it now I will never do it, and if I don't get my body into shape I will never bother to even go out and meet a man. Because men are turned on by what they see. And I just felt no-one would want to bother with me because I was frumpy and I had a double chin too – that's all gone now. I could go out now and flirt because I have confidence as a person. I like what I see in the mirror and I feel feminine, sexy and appealing.

In Rose's view, psychologists have invented emotional and interpersonal techniques which organise the practices of everyday life in accordance with such comforting notions of autonomous selfhood. Freedom has become synonymous with realising one's potential (i.e. the potential of the psychological self) through the activities in the everyday world and our daily lives. Rose's description of psychological therapies of normality and the disciplinary practices and techniques required for understanding and practising upon ourselves anticipates the form that psychological body image discourse takes on when it is reproduced in popular women's magazines (see Chapter 5):

> Psychology has invented . . . therapies of normality or the psychologies of everyday life, the pedagogies of self-fulfilment disseminated through the mass media, which translate enigmatic desires and dissatisfactions of the individual into precise ways of inspecting oneself, accounting for oneself, and working upon oneself in order to realize one's potential, gain happiness and exercise one's autonomy . . . to live as an autonomous individual, you must learn new techniques for understanding and practising upon yourself.
>
> (Rose 1996: 7)

Rose's work offers a way of understanding how women's bodies can be normalised and regulated through practices of subjectification that promise freedom, self-fulfilment and self-understanding. I use Rose's list of elements in modes of subjectification – problematizations, technologies, authorities and teleologies – to explore how the psychological discourse of body image produces women's bodies as pathological, within the broader discursive context of popular women's magazines (see Chapter 5).

Discourse analysis in social psychology

Discourse analysis offers a way of exploring how subjectivities, events and experiences are constituted in language. Varied styles of research have developed under the rubric 'discourse analysis' over recent years. Debates as to the definition, methods, purpose and scope of discourse analysis highlight the range of approaches available (e.g. Burman and Parker, 1993; Hollway, 1989; Potter and Wetherell, 1987). Approaches are characterised by important theoretical differences, which depend on how the boundary lines are drawn between different styles of work (Wetherell, 1996).

I take the approach of discourse analysis in social psychology as it has been developed by Margaret Wetherell, Jonathan Potter and Derek Edwards (see Potter and Edwards, 1992; Potter and Wetherell, 1987; Wetherell and Potter, 1992). This approach offers a tool for critical analysis of texts and talk compatible with my own critical feminist analysis of the production of women's bodies within a discourse of body image, in different empirical sites.

The discourse analytic approach developed by Wetherell *et al.* (above) draws critically and selectively on traditions as diverse as linguistic philosophy, rhetoric, ethnomethodology and conversation analysis, post-structuralism and developments in the sociology of scientific knowledge (see Potter and Wetherell, 1987, for an overview of the intellectual roots of a discourse approach; also Potter and Wetherell, 1994).

The action orientation of language

As discussed in Chapter 2, experimental psychology holds the view that language reflects already existing psychological and social realities. Language gets its meaning through a correspondence with objects or events in the external world. People's everyday talk (and writing) is taken to be a reflection of psychologically 'real' phenomena, such as personality traits, attitudes and cognitions, which are considered to be more or less stable over time. Body image researchers assume that attitudes and cognitions exist within the individual mind independent of language, and can be 'tapped into' with the appropriate methods of measurement.

Theoretical developments in traditions as diverse as ethnomethodology, literary theory and linguistic philosophy have highlighted the implausibility of a reflective view of language. Discourse analysis, having its roots in these traditions, is based on concepts of language and discourse which produce a different view of psychological processes and subjectivity from what has been historically envisioned in traditional psychology. The influence of ethnomethodology, and its interest in the 'doing' of gender and social life, has drawn the attention of discourse analysts to the functional, constructive nature of language. Language, in discourse analysis, is understood as action-oriented. That is, language constructs reality. Discourse analysis is concerned with what people 'do' with their talk and the types of resources that people draw on to construct objects, events, processes and experiences in particular ways.

The action-orientation of language is evident in ethnomethodology, where it has been suggested that 'people in conversations are constantly engaged in interpretive work to accomplish the meaning of utterances using their knowledge of context to help them' (Potter and Wetherell, 1987). Ethnomethodologists claim that how meaning becomes defined is dependent on context. They refer to this as 'the indexical property of discourse'. Generally speaking, indexical expressions are those expressions whose meaning alters with the context of their use (Barnes and Law, 1976). The contextual use of language in determining the meaning of expressions is relevant at a broader level for my analysis of body image discourse, and how it might be 'read' within the broader discursive context of popular women's magazines.

Discourse and interpretive repertoires

Wetherell and Potter (1992) emphasise the social practice of discourse use, taking a more flexible, practice-based view than Foucault. They also stress the context of use of discourse and, therefore, the 'act of discursive instantiation' (Wetherell and Potter, 1992: 90). This emphasis, they argue, first encourages the discourse analyst to treat the action orientation of discourse as primary, that is, the sense of any text or talk is derived from its situated use. Second, a focus on discourse as social practice has led to an analysis of discourse in everyday conversations and texts:

> This means that rather than attempting to derive 'discourses' from some set of materials, and then consider how those discourses work together and against one another in the abstract, the focus is very much on the implementation of those discourses in actual settings.
>
> (Wetherell and Potter, 1992: 90)

It is for these reasons that Wetherell and Potter prefer to use the term 'interpretive repertoires' rather than 'discourse' *per se* (see also Gilbert and Mulkay, 1984). The term 'interpretive repertoires' refers to:

> . . . broadly discernible clusters of terms, descriptions, and figures of speech often assembled around metaphors or vivid images . . . in more structuralist language we can talk of these things as systems of signification, such as the building blocks used for manufacturing versions of actions, self and social structures in talk. They are some of the resources for making evaluations, constructing factual versions and performing particular actions.
>
> (Wetherell and Potter, 1992: 91)

Interpretive repertoires are foremost a way of understanding the content of discourse and how that content is organised. The concern is with language use, that is, 'what is achieved by that use and the nature of interpretative resources that allow that achievement' (Wetherell and Potter, 1992: 91–2). Interpretive repertoires often act as sets of taken-for-granted frameworks of meaning that are in common use in a culture. These interpretive repertoires are often seen as 'common sense', with the effect that versions of events or experiences in their terms require no further explanation (Billig, 1987, 1991; Wetherell and Potter, 1992).

Discourse analysis emphasises the rhetorical basis of constructions of events, objects and subjectivities. This means that texts and talk are viewed as being organised in specific ways which make a particular reality appear 'real' – that is, solid and factual. People draw on a variety of techniques and devices to accomplish this effect of realism in their accounts and can be more or less successful in this task (see Edwards and Potter, 1992).

Highlighting the rhetorical function of account construction emphasises how accounts are not only constructed to form an argument but are also constructed *against* alternatives (Billig, 1987, 1991). A focus on rhetorical function draws attention to the ways that a particular version or argument is constructed to undermine competing alternatives. Popular women's magazines, in their reproduction of body image discourse, provide excellent examples of the rhetorical strategies and devices employed by publishers to construct a particular story about women's 'body image problems' (see Chapter 4 and especially Chapter 5).

To say that subjectivity is constituted through discourse means that '*who one is and what one is like*' is established through discursive acts (Wetherell and Potter, 1992: 78). Subjectivity, discursively constituted, is not unitary or fixed, but constituted and reconstituted in talk and text in social practice (Wetherell and White, 1992).

Discourse does not play a facilitative role in which some pre-discursive, pre-constituted 'identity' is expressed. Rather, it is argued that 'the forms of subjectivity that become instantiated in discourse at any given moment should be seen as sedimentation of past discursive practices' (Wetherell and Potter, 1992: 78). In this view, subjectivity is constructed from the interpretive repertoires (the stories and narratives of identity) in circulation in our culture. Interpretive repertoires set up subject positions that offer or provide people with a sense of identity. Due to educational, cultural and social conditions, some subject positions are more readily available to some people than others.

In the next three empirical chapters, a discourse analytic approach informs my examination of different empirical sites where women's bodies are produced within a discourse of body image. In Chapter 4, I use a descriptive form of discourse analysis. In Chapters 5 and 6, my analyses are based on close readings of the text and I identify the interpretive repertoires structuring the texts and look at the potential effects of these for women's bodies.

In the next chapter, I use a descriptive form of discourse analysis, based on readings of one article about women and 'body image' featured in *More*, a popular women's magazine (Morris, 1992). I offer readings of the article and the text in which it is embedded, examining the strategies the magazine employs to present potentially transgressive ideas about 'body image' in a way that fits the publishers' commercial goals, and which reproduce body image as a central organising feature of women's understandings of our/themselves.

4

'WHAT OTHER WOMEN LOOK LIKE NAKED' – READING A POPULAR WOMEN'S MAGAZINE

I was incredulous when I first saw this issue of *More* magazine, 'dedicated' to women's body image. I was taken aback by the magazine's promise to show me what naked women 'really' look like. I felt I had wandered into the wrong section of the bookstore. The 'body image' article, juxtaposed with the usual fare of popular women's health and beauty magazines, appeared to be an anomaly. However, this was just one of the first of numerous articles devoted to the topic of women's body image problems that have been appearing in women's magazines since then (see Chapter 5). This chapter is a critical analysis of that issue of *More* magazine. I utilize a descriptive form of discourse analysis to examine the ways in which the magazine's publishers present information related to the 'problem' of women's body image within the context of a magazine dedicated to the promotion of an homogenized ideal of feminine beauty.

Popular women's magazines are the biggest selling of all magazine categories. In New Zealand in the first 6 months of 1998, the top three women's magazines (published weekly) sold nearly 364,000 copies.[1] *Marie Claire* magazine (USA) was selling 948,321 copies in 2000, with a world-wide readership of 15,000,000. *Cosmopolitan* magazine boasts a world-wide readership of 35,000,000.[2] Because women are the primary purchasers of goods and services, the magazine industry is a particularly lucrative market for advertisers, especially in the areas of food and cosmetics, which are the two largest advertising categories in women's magazines (see McCracken, 1993). As a result, advertising makes up almost the entire content of women's magazines, occupying up to 95% of space in some magazines. Delineation between advertising and editorial content has become so blurred that it is often difficult to distinguish the two, as advertising increasingly shapes editorial content (McCracken, 1993).

Women's magazines function as an 'ostensibly authoritative text of femininity' (Smith, 1990). Their overwhelming focus on themes of personal change and self-improvement constitute a 'discourse of femininity', where a woman's body is regarded as permanently flawed and always in need of remedial work. Feelings of insecurity and self-dissatisfaction, which are the *sine qua non* of the advertising industry, and which fuel consumerism, are induced by ubiquitous glossy images of perfect-looking, ideal women (McCracken, 1993).

The strategy of inducing anxiety and dissatisfaction is what Roland Barthes (1973) refers to as 'the promise of the future self'. This 'future self', a crucial presence in advertising, functions through the perceived discrepancy between who we are now and who we can be in the future (McCracken, 1993). The 'we' addressed in popular women's magazines are almost entirely white, Western women. Contemporary images of the ideal and desirable future self are embodied in (usually artificially created) representations of women who are white, flawless, thin and toned. When compared to women's actual bodies – which are never the ideal – these representations can instil a sense of inadequacy in women.

Solutions are offered for inadequacy, to solve the dissatisfaction created. Alongside images of smooth, hairless and slim women are advertisements for products which smooth wrinkles, remove 'unwanted' hair and reduce 'excess' weight, for example. Desire is created by the perceived deficiencies of a woman's actual body in relation to the ideal image that is presented to the reader as her objective. Paradoxically, women tend to experience this desire as pleasure. Magazines are bought 'as a treat'; the images seem to offer the pleasurable fantasy of relatively easily attained (just buy this!) self-improvement and beauty. This creates 'the circuit: image–desire–shopping' (Smith, 1990). In this way, magazines provide multiple pleasures for women with messages that conflate desire and consumerism (McCracken, 1993; Smith, 1990; see also Gough-Yates, 2003).

Women's magazines also contribute to what counts as common sense about women's bodies. It seems 'normal' that women should have hairless legs and flat stomachs – although all women have 'naturally' hairy legs and most have not-flat stomachs, these things are seen as unusual (and 'unnatural'). Advertisers and publishers try to establish such common-sense views and preferred meanings of reality in order to sell commodities (McCracken, 1993; Smith, 1990; Winship, 1987).

More magazine and 'real' bodies

Women's magazines are almost completely dominated by images of perfect, idealised bodies. It is almost never the case that 'real' bodies (i.e. non-model and/or non-'made-up' bodies) are displayed there – except in 'before' and 'after' features, which illustrate precisely how a product can 'remedy' the 'problems' women 'have' with their flawed bodies.

However, in the early 1990s, *More*, a leading New Zealand magazine, published an article headed, 'Naked Truths: A special report: what other women look like naked – women talk about their bodies' (Loates, 1992: 43). The article included black and white photographs of naked women who were not models, accompanied by interviews in which these women commented on what they liked and disliked about their bodies. Two other magazines had already published similar stories not long before, and had attracted my curiosity. I wondered why women's magazines were suddenly showing the naked bodies of 'ordinary' women.

More magazine's publishers, through the editor's introduction, claimed that the article would be 'comforting' to women, and show them that they are 'normal', just like everyone else. The editorial implied that 'normal' is 'what we all are' and that 'normal' is acceptable. Assuming that the publishers would not run such a feature if it threatened to jeopardise either readership or advertising revenue, the question begs to be asked, how does *More* handle what appears to be a contradiction between its readers' 'normal' bodies and the idealised representations of women's bodies featured in their magazine? On the one hand, the 'real' body is presented as 'normal' in the article, and on the other, the magazine is dependent on women seeing their 'normal' bodies precisely as not-normal, and in need of remedy.

This chapter focuses closely on the question of the tensions between contradictory discourses within this issue of *More*. The analysis illustrates ways women might read the article on 'Naked Truths' (about themselves), and the implications of these readings for women's experiences of their bodies. As argued in Chapter 3, research that focuses on the discursive constitution of subjectivities can inform understandings of how particular versions of reality are constructed by texts, and what are the possible functions and effects of these constructions on women's everyday lives. In this research, I focus specifically on women's magazines because they can be understood as a significant site of production of women's bodies/subjectivities. There are limited sets of often contradictory meanings (e.g. about 'women's bodies' and 'femininity') to be found in popular women's magazines, and these represent the dominant meanings available in the current socio-historical moment.

A form of descriptive discourse analysis has been used here as a tool to examine the strategies *More* employs which both reproduce women's bodies as flawed and in need of improvement, while simultaneously positioning the magazine as progressive and supportive of women. This sort of analysis allows a systemic understanding that goes beyond 'self-evident' constructions, such as those apparent in many women's magazines that emphasise individual freedom, choice and power.

My discussion of how women might read the *More* article is based on a close reading of the text of 'Naked Truths' and the editor's introduction (Morris, 1992). I do three readings (see discussion of discourse analysis in Chapter 3). The first and second are immediate, common-sense responses, a 'collage' generated from my own experiences as a young pakeha (New Zealand European) woman magazine reader, and those of some of my peers with whom I discussed the text in detail. The third is a critical reading of the editor's 'scene setting' and the effects this might have on readers.

Before I present the readings, I will provide more information about the context of the article 'Naked Truths'. *More* magazine's circulation in 1992 was 75,000. *More*, which amalgamated with an Australian women's magazine to become

She&More in 1996, was published monthly and belonged to the 'health and beauty' genre of women's magazines. This genre is characterised by the promotion of a physical ideal for women, where health and beauty are seen as synonymous. Other aspects of women/women's lives (such as job satisfaction, financial questions) are undervalued or ignored at the same time as a concern with physical appearance is exaggerated (McCracken, 1993). The central theme, consistently relayed, is that a woman's potential can primarily be realised through her physical appearance. As with the other magazines of its genre, *More* promotes ideals of fashion and beauty and the image of woman as white, young, thin and heterosexual. The achievement of an ideal standard of beauty, in these magazines as in most other sites of representation of women, is primarily linked with romantic heterosexuality; with getting and keeping a man (Bordo, 1993a; McCracken, 1993; Wetherell and White, 1992).

An image that typifies this ideal, and which is repeated in essence on virtually every page in *More*, is reproduced in an advertisement for Estée Lauder's 'Spellbound' perfume. This double-page advertisement appears on the inside front cover of *More* (October, 1992) which features 'Naked Truths' and shows a perfect woman who has a man 'spellbound'. As readers and voyeurs, we are invited to study her flawless skin and shape, and to believe that her perfect body (along with some perfume) is enough to attract and keep a man and therefore for the woman (women) to be happy, satisfied, successful and complete.

Of the 155 pages in this issue of *More*, 102 are devoted to similar advertising in some form, that is, nearly 70% of the magazine. Products advertised include:

> Immunage UV Defense System: 15 times more protective in your fight against wrinkles . . . so skin is protected and moisturised. Looks younger, prettier, day after day

> Shiseido Fair Beauty Illuminated UV White Compact with UV filters. Apply wet or dry for a natural, flawless finish

> Nivea Visage: What does she have that is so special? Some people have a certain look that sets them apart. Nivea Visage will give your skin all the help it needs to stay supple and youthful

and, placed after the article on body image, an advertisement for a weight-loss product:

> Slimmers Choice Yoghurt, 100% natural: Life's a long road, it's only natural to not carry excess baggage.

It is within this context that *More* published the article on women's body image. The article incorporates a brief editorial about women and their bodies by the sub-editor, followed by photographs of 10 women, naked and with their faces blanked out. Beneath the photographs are the women's ages, height, weight, detailed body measurements and clothing size. These are the bodies of 'ordinary' women, a range of body shapes and sizes but all would be considered either overweight or out of proportion in comparison with the 'model' bodies shown in *More* magazine. Alongside these photographs of the women's headless bodies are two half-page columns entitled, 'WHERE THE BOYS ARE on the subject of women's bodies', with comments from four men about what they like and don't like about women's bodies.

The header, below, introduces readers to the article:

> In our hearts, we know there's no such thing as the perfect body. There's beauty in every shape and size. Yet in our critical mind's eye, some bodies are more perfect than others, and it's usually our own that comes off second best in the comparison game – that is, until you talk to other women about it: then you begin to realise that we all share the same fears and harbour the same desires. Lyn Loates [the author of the article] puts the average, normal female body in focus.
>
> (Loates, 1992: 43)

The introduction ends by telling us, 'it (your body) is unique and that uniqueness deserves to be celebrated' (Loates, 1992: 43).

Readings 1 and 2: overview

For Readings 1 and 2 (in italics) below, I, as a magazine reader, leafed through the magazine, looking briefly at the advertisements and editorial material, then focused on the body image article for a short while before reading the editor's introduction more closely. I then recorded my 'common-sense' impression of both the images and the editorial – one which might characterise the response of a young, casual reader. This reading (1 and 2 below) offers one way of understanding or interpreting the body image feature within the magazine, and is a representation of the consensus of my own views and those of women peers, both Maori and New Zealand European, with whom I discussed the article.[3]

Reading 1

Reading this article, it was initially the photographs themselves that had the most impact on me. I got a real shock when I saw those pictures, particularly because they are such a sharp contrast to the coloured glossy pictures in the rest of the magazine. They looked really grim in comparison. I'm just not used to seeing pictures of women who are really overweight with lots of cellulite standing there naked. The women look as if they're in an identity parade for 'suspects'; their faces are blanked out and they are all standing in the same position – sort of frozen and lifeless. Compared to the pictures in the rest of the magazine, these women, even the thin ones, looked awful. Like I thought, 'I know who I'd rather look like and it's not them'. When I look at the images of the real women in black and white I don't see that they have a life. Really all I can see from the photos of their bodies is where they physically start and finish. They seem to be just for looking at and comparing myself to. I looked at some of those women's bodies and then looked at their height and weight measurements and a couple of times I got a real shock because I weigh the same as some of them and I thought, 'God, do I look like that?' Because if I do, then I actually look much worse than I thought.

When I looked at the colour pictures on the other pages, I felt a sense of relief. Although I know they're models and they use air-brushing, etc. to make them look really good, they looked much more real to me. Of course, they're photographed in exotic locations and all that but it's the women's facial expressions that draw me in, that seem to tell me about her . . . her pose, her smile, her enigmatic expression. It's as if she is there for me, looking at me, telling me something – seducing me? Yes . . . many of the expressions on these women's faces are those you'd expect to be reserved for a lover. In these photos the woman is always doing something – in the process of being – I can tell she has a life, a deep inner life, an emotional life. I can look at those pictures, look into her eyes and she seems to have something or be in possession of something – this 'something' is a mystery but I know that I want it . . . I want to know what that secret is . . . I want to know what her secret is.

Reading 2

The Editor's introduction

The editor's words are set out in italic type.

Think about this for a minute. If someone asked you to describe the way you look, what would you say? As if I don't spend most of my time thinking about it – I don't need to be asked to think about it.

Now think about what your close friends or lover would say if asked the same question about you. Do the replies match up? Of course my friends and my lover would say I look all right, but that's half the trouble – if they didn't say that, if they were honest, then maybe I'd do something about the way I look.

If you're a woman, chances are, your own description will be much more critical. No, it's just more honest. I know only too well what my own body looks like – I know how much weight I've put on in the last few months.

Despite the fact that most bodies are perfectly normal, it's the perfect part that trips us up. My body is definitely not perfectly normal. It doesn't look the way other women's bodies look – in magazines, on TV – friends' bodies.

Somehow we imagine other women must be firmer, fitter, or more shapely than we are. It's not that I imagine that other bodies are fitter or firmer, I know they are. Lots of women have flat stomachs and thin thighs.

That's why we've dedicated nearly a dozen pages this month to the way women treat their bodies. It's an issue which affects the quality of so many lives right now. Tragic stories about eating disorders such as anorexia and bulimia are not rare; many have been published in this magazine. I'm not like those women that starve themselves – if only I had some of their self-control. I only need to lose 6 kilos – 7 would be great – that's all. I've tried throwing up but I just can't do it . . . I envy Lisa and Jo who can just pig out and then vomit it all up – having their cake and eating it too.

Exercise obsession is one of the hang-ups of the '90's. Exercise obsession – yeah, right! – I have enough trouble trying to make myself go to the gym or go for a run . . .

. . . but that's not the full story. There are also women who love going to the gym because it makes them feel fit, strong and alive. They know that being the right weight for their height means better health. It's not as if this is news to me. I know all this stuff. I know it makes a difference. I've just got to try even harder with my exercise – redouble my efforts . . . I remember that time when I was doing the Jane Fonda workout four times a week and running for 50 minutes every morning – I felt great, I was on such a high – but I can't seem to get back into it . . .

We all achieve peace of mind in different ways. Maybe you prefer to relax on the sofa with a good book instead of pounding the pavement in running shoes – it doesn't matter. Yeah . . . the trouble is I spend too much time lying on the couch knowing I should be out running . . . usually when I read, I eat as well – the two seem to go together. Of course it matters that I don't run or exercise because I get fat and feel sluggish and get even more depressed about the way I look, especially because I know I only have myself to blame.

Feeling positive and happy with yourself radiates through your whole being. The point is, if you feel good on the inside, you look good on the outside – and both those things affect the state of your health and happiness (more on this in part two of our special report, next month). How can I feel good on the inside when I look like this on the outside? I know that if I lost weight and got back to the weight I was last summer then I would feel better about myself. When I'm at that weight I'm happier, more confident and I feel more like going out and doing things.

Most of the available statistics published on body image have been collected overseas and it's not always possible to apply them directly to New Zealand. Naomi Wolf says in The Beauty Myth *that 25% of women are on a diet on any given day, with 50% finishing, breaking or starting one. That's scary. Is it really true of New Zealand women? Surely our collective self-esteem can't be that bad?* I wish I was in the 25% of women who are on a diet – I just want to find one that works that I can stick to so that I can start to feel better about myself. If I didn't look like this then I wouldn't feel so bad about myself. Everyone knows that you feel better about yourself when you're not carrying extra weight.

American writer Cris Evatt recently published a book called He & She: 60 Significant Differences Between Men and Women, *in which it's said that 68% of men like the way they look when naked, compared with only 29% of women.* Everyone knows it's not the same for men – they don't have to worry about their weight in the same way that we do. Most of them aren't fat anyway and it doesn't seem to worry the ones that are – look at Stephen – he still has girlfriends even though he's really quite fat. His friends don't think any the worse of him because he's not thin. It's just not as important for men as it is for women.

Most of the women who appear in advertisements and magazines wearing the latest fashions and swimsuits are, of course, models. Their bodies are their business – they work at them. I envy those models because that's all they have to do – all they have to worry about. They can work out, exercise and run and it's all part of their work really – sort of like their nine-to-five job I suppose.

But that's not the reality for most of the rest of us, and we know it. What I need to do is to really make a determined effort to get in shape – like make it the absolute priority in my life, the most important thing – it's like that sometimes but then I seem to slip – I need to do what Jane Fonda used to do – she'd imagine she was a professional dancer who had to perform in public so it was essential that she worked out every day.

She'd put on her legwarmers and her leotard and really go for it – as if she were practising for a performance that night. I need to be that disciplined. I could do it. Probably the only way to really get myself back on track with this weight thing is to be totally dedicated to really changing my body. I know that's not how it is for me at the moment but I know I could do it . . . it would mean changing some things in my life and I'd need to really make myself do it . . .

Men know it too, judging by the comments they've made to accompany our special report. At least the men were honest – said what they thought – not like Michael (lover) – it sounds like some of them are talking about my body the way it is now – yeah it's almost as if they know what I look like . . .

Any woman who's been in a gym or swimming-pool changing room will tell you that it's very satisfying to compare yourself with other normal everyday women – not for the purposes of one-upmanship, but because we're all different and we all have parts of our bodies we like or loathe. I must be going to the wrong gym, I always see women who look better than I do. There are lots of women at the gym with really good bodies – really toned and slim. I often come away feeling really depressed and down on myself because I don't match up to them at all. Especially the ones who walk around naked in the showers – I can't believe that they don't feel good about their bodies.

It's comforting to realise that all those dynamic, interesting and great-looking women you see walking around every day are just like us underneath. I'm not like them. Those women are in another league altogether and I'll never look anything like them unless I get a grip on my eating and really do something about the way I look.

It was in the same spirit that we asked 10 very different women to tell us how they felt about themselves naked – a personal question, and one we weren't sure anyone would be brave enough to answer – but not only did we find women who were proud to show us their own bodies and talk about them, others also wanted to join the conversation and put their point of view and that became part of the story too. It might be okay for those women to look like that, that's fine for them – but there's no way I want to look like that. There's no way in the world I'd want to be photographed for that article – God – some of them look really terrible. Much fatter than I am. No wonder their faces are blanked out. It's really awful seeing them because looking at them I can see what I might look like if I don't do something about my weight now . . . I could just go on getting bigger and bigger and bigger . . . Yuk. They might be proud of themselves but I would feel really ashamed to look like that – I would be really, really miserable. In a way it's quite good to see those pictures because it might just give me enough of a fright to really do something about the way I look at the moment.

In revealing their bodies, these women also reveal their attitudes and pride in themselves, I think most of us will recognise ourselves in there somewhere. My God, I just don't believe those fat women feel good about themselves or proud of themselves – and it is obvious from some of their comments about their bodies that they're not that happy with the way they look. I don't think that they realised what they were doing, agreeing to be photographed. Of course the thin ones wouldn't be worried about it because they look the way they're supposed to look – so it wouldn't be a problem for them – just an opportunity to show off.

Reading 3:
Critical analysis of the editor's introduction

In this reading, I look at the way the editor's introduction is constructed and how it functions to achieve the reading above. I chose to 'read' and analyse the editor's introduction because she is at the interface between readers, publishers and advertisers. It is her job to ensure that the magazine stays afloat. As editor she is part of the 'brand' of the magazine. She addresses her readers with an assumed objectivity and offers common-sense advice and information in the spirit of friendship (McCracken, 1993). The editor decides what to include in the magazine and tells readers what they will be interested in reading. In her introduction she sets the scene for how women will read what follows in the magazine (Russell, personal communication, 1993).

Think about this for a minute. If someone asked you to describe the way you look, what would you say? Now think about what your close friends or lover would say if asked the same question about you. Do the replies match up? Asking women to describe the way they look and compare their own judgement to that of others normalises woman's body as an object of scrutiny, promoting self-criticism and self-surveillance, and positioning women as passive recipients of others' gaze and judgement. The first two sentences encourage a self-consciousness that comes from stepping outside 'one's own skin' to 'objectively' describe what you see. Women are encouraged to think about what others think about their bodies and privilege external judgements over their own. The editor's opening question implies the existence or operation of an external referent, that is, a norm or a standard against which a woman can measure herself and against which she can describe her body.

If you're a woman, chances are, your own description will be much more critical. The operation of an external referent is strengthened by this sentence. It is claimed that when *women* look at themselves they will find fault with what they see. This statement implies that we are critical of our looks because we are women – self-criticism is both 'natural' and inescapable, rather than, for example, a product of contemporary (and historical) notions of the female body as flawed or deviant. This statement depicts women's bodies as problematic, undermines women's authority and expertise in relation to their own bodies and casts doubt on women's ability to 'know' their own bodies. It suggests that there is a correct way of seeing 'women's bodies' and a woman's view (*'much more critical'*) is somehow wrong and invalid.

The editor suggests women's self-criticism is irrational. There are a number of places in her introduction where she brings women's rationality into question. In the opening paragraph, above, a woman's ability to give a reasonable description of herself is disputed. Further on, the editor claims women irrationally *'imagine'* other women must be firmer, fitter or more shapely than we are.

Women are good at being hard on themselves. This statement is blaming of individual women but this accusation is lightened by saying we are good at being hard on ourselves, rather than that we are actually bad because we do this. This statement resonates with the notion of 'womanly virtue' – that is, 'being hard on themselves' is something women as a group do, a truism about women. If she had written instead, 'Women are hard on themselves', this would have been empathic and perhaps invited further comment as to why this might be so.

Despite the fact that most bodies are perfectly normal, it's the perfect part that trips us up. In this strong appeal to common-sense knowledge, saying that *most* bodies are perfectly normal creates a gap for women to position themselves outside of perfectly normal. When the *Concise Oxford Dictionary* definition of 'normal' – 'usual, typical, conforming to standard' – is applied, then 'normal' refers to ubiquitous, homogenised images of 'model' women seen in magazines such as *More*. The pairing of the disparate terms *'perfectly'* and *'normal'* illustrates the contradictions implied. There is no such thing as perfectly normal. Perfectly normal is not perfect, it is just normal. In the context of this magazine, referring to 'ordinary' women's bodies as *'perfectly normal'* is disingenuous and misleading. What the editor is saying is that most bodies are imperfectly normal. This interpretation is strengthened when she says, *'it's the "perfect" part that trips us up'*. Understandably so – it is only the models who look perfect. The reader is positioned as not knowing what is going on, not knowing what is perfectly normal, not knowing what is 'real'.

Somehow we imagine other women must be firmer, fitter or more shapely than we are. The word '*somehow*' disavows *More*'s important role in women's imagining that other women are firmer, fitter and more shapely than they are. The most ubiquitous sources of comparison for women are images of the ideal body *More* proliferates. In addition, using the word '*imagine*' in this context denies women's lived experience and implies that it is 'all in our mind'. To say that women '*imagine*' this places responsibility for this 'flawed' thinking with women themselves. This suggests that the problems women have with body image occur in a vacuum, rather than in a specific historical and cultural context (and particularly the context of the magazine). It also implies that women are unable to separate the imagined from the real.

That's why we've dedicated nearly a dozen pages this month to the way women treat their bodies. The word '*dedicated*' evokes notions of devotion and integrity and gives the impression that *More* is supporting women and doing something beneficial for women by publishing this feature. This sentence eclipses the fact that women have paid $5.00 for this magazine, over 70% of which is dedicated to selling women products and services to remedy flaws in their appearance – this includes a full-page advertisement for a weight-loss product. The use of the word '*treat*' in this context has negative connotations, for example, ill-treat and mistreat, and is blaming of individual women.

It's an issue which affects the quality of so many lives right now. Tragic stories about eating disorders such as anorexia and bulimia are not rare; many have been published in this magazine. Exercise obsession is one of the hang-ups of the '90's . . . but that's not the full story. This paragraph is central to the editor's construction of a standard story about body image, notably through the operation of the disclaimer '*but that's not the full story*', which contextualises the other comments she makes. The editor tells us the way women treat their bodies is an issue but does not clarify exactly what the issue is, so it remains somewhat obscure what it is she is addressing. In saying, '*the way women treat their bodies is affecting the quality of so many lives right now*', the editor removes this issue from the socio-historical context of anorexia and bulimia, positioning it in the immediate present, particular to contemporary women's lives. This gives the impression that eating disorders are a 'fad' and not something that might or will continue to be a serious issue for women in the future.

Mentioning only anorexia and bulimia omits the experiences of many other women who would not be diagnosed with an eating disorder but who experience distress about eating and the size and shape of their bodies.

The editor points out *More*'s awareness of this topical issue, positioning the magazine as both progressive in printing these stories and supportive of women in running this article on body image. Describing these difficulties as a 'hang-up' and 'an obsession' implies individual pathology, that is, these problems are something that happens to and is located within individual women, rather than a product of social processes. The disclaimer *'but that's not the full story'* says, 'yes, it is serious, but no, it's not' – and lightens the seriousness of the problem. To say that this is not the full story suggests there has been some concealment of the truth.

There are also women who love going to the gym because it makes them feel fit, strong and alive. They recognise that being the right weight for their height means better health. It is important to note that the editor is addressing all women here, including the women in the body image article. The bodies shown in the body image article are positioned as 'transgressive', because they clearly are not the *'right weight for their height'*, and thus outside the group of *'fit, strong and alive'* women the editor refers to above. Both women in the black and white photographs and readers who look like them are framed as women who have failed to recognise that *'being the right weight for their height means better health'*. This implies that they are not 'healthy' and therefore not attractive, given the current aesthetics of health, whereby a woman's health is predicated on her appearance, and health is equated with beauty (Spitzack, 1990). On the other hand, those women who do attend the gym and who recognise that *'being the right weight for their height'* means better health are granted superior moral virtue. *'Being the right weight for their height'* is a euphemism for slimness, given the normalising properties of height/weight scales.

We all achieve peace of mind in different ways. This sentence reinforces the common-sense notion *'being the right weight for one's height means better health'*, established in the previous paragraph, and at the same time extends the equation by linking *'being the right weight for one's height'* with peace of mind. This sentence ties in attendance at the gym with peace of mind.

Maybe you prefer to relax on the sofa with a good book instead of pounding the pavement in running shoes – it doesn't matter. After the two previous lines it is not convincing that it really doesn't matter whether women *'relax on the sofa'* or *'pound the pavement'*. The two images are unequal and morally laden. What the editor is saying is that it *DOES* matter. It has been stated that those who attend the gym are, by virtue of their behaviour, '*fit, strong and alive*' and that recognising that '*being the right weight for your height means better health*'. Therefore, those women who do this occupy the moral high ground.

Feeling positive and happy with yourself radiates through your whole being. The point is, if you feel good on the inside, you look good on the outside – and both these things affect the state of your health and happiness. A central theme underpinning the visual and verbal text of *More* is that if you look good, you will feel good. This theme is inverted here with the editor telling women that '*if you feel good on the inside you look good on the outside*'. Given the dominant message of the magazine, that a woman's physical appearance is the most important factor in achieving happiness and contentment, this inversion is very unstable. Throughout *More* magazine, the conflation of beauty and health reinforces an aesthetics of health based on physical attractiveness.

Most of the available statistics on body image have been collected overseas and it's not always possible to apply them directly to New Zealand. Naomi Wolf says in The Beauty Myth *that 25% of women are on a diet on any given day, with 50% finishing, breaking or starting one. That's scary. Is it really true of NZ women? Surely our collective self-esteem can't be that bad?* The editor introduces these statistics by calling into question their relevance to *More*'s readers. This minimises and casts doubt on the seriousness and pervasiveness of dieting behaviour. The editor appeals to the reader to deny that the statistics are true. In the context of what has been said above, this question is rhetorical. Her reaction to these statistics, 'That's scary', is overplayed and serves as a strategy of denial. The final sentence, '*surely our collective self-esteem can't be that bad*', functions as a disclaimer – this is a problem but it isn't a problem. The use of the word '*collective*' has an homogenising function and suggests that we are all in this together, that the editor is one of us. This encourages readers to identify with the editor and therefore with her views. Again, the editor provides an individualistic explanation for 'body image' problems. She claims that dieting is the province of individual women with 'bad self-esteem'.

American writer Cris Evatt recently published a book called He & She: 60 Significant Differences Between Men and Women, *in which it's said that 68% of men like the way they look when naked compared with only 29% of women.* Following Wolf's statistics with this quote about '*differences between men and women*' reinforces the common-sense notion that women's dislike of their bodies can be attributed to their biological sex. This suggests that these differences are natural and intractable.

Most of the women who appear in advertisements and magazines wearing the latest fashions and swimsuits are, of course, models. ALL, not *'most'*, women who appear in advertisements wearing the latest fashions and swimsuits are models. The word 'most' allows the possibility that some of the women we see in the magazine are like us; that is, they are not models but 'ordinary' women. At the same time, *'of course'* functions to reinforce common-sense knowledge that models are not like ordinary women. This introduces some confusion as to the demarcation between 'ordinary' women and 'model' women and increases the likelihood that women will believe that what they see, the ideal image, is attainable.

Their bodies are their business – they work at them. This explanation as to why these models look the way they do leaves space for women to make the link between *'hard work'* and the ideal body and to believe that it is possible to look like these models if we *'work hard'* enough at our bodies. It connects with the editor's comments about women who go to the gym because *'they recognise that being the right weight for their height means better health'*. Giving strength to this interpretation is the omission of other factors that are pivotal in achieving the 'model' body, for example, the age of the model (pubescent in many cases), the high incidence of bulimia and anorexia amongst models, drug-induced weight loss, photographic techniques such as air-brushing, lighting, and the use of face and body make-up. Nor is there any mention of how images of the 'ideal' body are produced via the practice of using body parts of individual models (e.g. the hands of one model and the legs of another in an image of a woman putting on stockings).

But that's not the reality for most of the rest of us and we know it. 'Most of the rest of us' don't work at our bodies but some of us do. This implies that some ordinary women who are not models have achieved bodies like models through making their bodies their business and working hard at them.

Men know it too, judging by the comments they've made to accompany our special report. The following quote from 'Kevin' typifies the comments made by all the men:

> 'The way to work out whether a woman is sexy or not is to think about what she'd look like without clothes. If you're still interested in taking a look, then she's sexy. Overall I rate personality higher than body. Even the best body in the world wouldn't help a horrible personality. But, now that I think about it, the best personality couldn't save a nightmare body either' (Kevin, 31, writer).

Including men's comments about women's bodies reinforces women's bodies as objects of the male gaze, increases women's self-consciousness and supports the central themes underpinning the visual and verbal text of *More* outlined above (e.g. compulsory heterosexuality, women's bodies as sexualised objects of a male gaze, men as the arbiters of women's bodies).

Any woman who's been in a gym or swimming-pool changing room will tell you that it's very satisfying to compare yourself with other normal, everyday women – not for the purposes of one-upmanship, but because we're all different and we all have parts of our bodies we like or loathe. It's comforting to realise that all those dynamic, interesting and great-looking women you see walking around every day are just like us, underneath. Phrases like '*Any woman . . .*' and '*we all have*' are appeals to common sense. In this context, comparison is considered normal and natural; we all judge our own bodies in comparison to others. That this comparison is described as '*very satisfying*' suggests a certain amount of one-upmanship, a competitive element. The editor says that we're all different, but in *More* difference is framed as transgressive, that is, not conforming to the 'ideal' body. In the next sentence she gives us permission to hate our bodies ('*we all have parts of our bodies we like or loathe*') and normalises the cultural fragmentation and objectification of women's bodies. This fragmentation potentially encourages women to consume beauty products by focusing on particular aspects of their bodies as problematic and in need of specialised products. '*Loathe*' is a powerfully emotive word to describe and normalise women's feelings for their bodies. After telling that us we are all different, she assures us that the '*great-looking women*' we see walking around everyday are '*just like us underneath*'. This claim is potentially belied by comparison between our 'normal, everyday' bodies and the 'ideal' bodies presented as the norm in *More*.

It was in the same spirit that we asked 10 very different women to tell us how they felt about themselves naked . . . Here difference is problematic for women. Because we do not have any other information about the women (e.g. employment, political views, interests, etc.) that would differentiate them for us, 'different' refers to physical differences between the women in the article, and between those women and the 'model' women in the magazine. The photographs in the article, in the context of this magazine, point up difference from the ideal, deviance from the norm of the 'model' women.

. . . – a personal question and one we weren't sure anyone would be brave enough to answer . . . This statement, suggesting that *More* believes

women do not feel comfortable or confident about their bodies, evidences both the construction and normalising of women's relationship to their bodies as one of loathing. Other interpretations of women's reticence to talk about their bodies and to appear naked in *More*, for example personal privacy or lack of interest, are absent.

. . . but not only did we find women who were proud to show us their own bodies and talk about them, others also wanted to join the conversation and put their point of view and that became part of the story, too. In revealing their bodies these women also reveal their attitudes and pride in themselves. The '*pride*' the editor claims these women feel in publicly revealing their bodies is contradicted by the presentation of the women, with the blanked-out faces. Pride is nowhere evident in the anonymity of the women and the self-deprecating comments many of the women made about their bodies, for example: 'My bum is my least favourite part. It's too big, but I don't do anything about it'; 'There's a lot about my body I would change if I could'; 'I could handle the rest of my body if my breasts would just shrink a bit'. There is also the unspoken idea that if these were the 10 women in New Zealand that *More* found who were '*proud*' to show their bodies and they feel less than happy with themselves, what do the other women who were not proud enough to reveal their bodies feel about themselves?

I think most of us will recognise ourselves in there somewhere. We can compare our own bodies *vis-à-vis* the 'ideal' body and against these 'ordinary' women's bodies and recognise ourselves in the latter group, that is, other than ideal. We recognise ourselves as 'not-ideal', as outside the norm, as wanting or lacking.

There are several points that can be made here in summary. First, why did *More* publish, at this historical moment, what they implied was a potentially radical article featuring 'ordinary' women naked. Women's bodies are a topical issue. As the advertisers know, they sell (Goldstein, 1991). A contributing factor in the publication of this article may have been the greater interest in alternative, critical discourses of 'beauty' and 'femininity' that draw attention to how an 'ideal' of physical appearance for women sustains not only billion dollar 'beauty' and advertising industries but also dominant power relations between men and women (e.g. Naomi Wolf's' *The Beauty Myth*, 1990). In not running this article, *More* might have risked appearing non-progressive alongside its sister magazines.

The potentially transgressive nature of this article is another reason why it may have been featured at this time. As feminist ideas become more accepted, even common-sense, the photographs and interviews with 'ordinary' women can, possibly, be read as positive – women transgressing dominant social norms of physical appearance. Publishing photographs of 'ordinary' women naked might point out the 'difference' between 'ordinary' women and 'ideal' women in such a way as to highlight the impossibility of achieving that 'ideal'.

Magazine publishers have, historically, attempted to harness transgressive elements (in this case the bodies of 'ordinary' women) in their own interests. One way of doing this has been to encourage readers to enjoy certain marginalised differences or pleasures and then find a way of containing them by tying them to consumerism (see Bordo, 1993a; McCracken, 1993). Obviously a groundswell of 'self-acceptance' among women would potentially threaten the publishers' commercial goals. If 'ordinary' women accept and value themselves as they are, they will not spend millions of dollars to 'improve' themselves by correcting bodily 'flaws' (Spitzack, 1990). Including the 'Naked Truths' article in the context of a fashion and beauty magazine such as *More* provides the magazine's publishers with the challenge of presenting 'ordinary' women's bodies in such a way as to fit with the commercial goals of the magazine.

The commercial goals of *More* are supported by its advertising and editorial material. This material maintains a system of mutually sustaining themes – a woman's body is her most valuable commodity *and* the most flawed aspect of her being. As a business enterprise, *More*'s financial survival depends on women purchasing products advertised in the magazine. In this issue of *More*, the circuit image–desire–shopping is created through the juxtaposition of 'ordinary' women's bodies and 'model' bodies. Consciously or subconsciously, comparing their own bodies to 'ideal' bodies creates the desire for improvement. Showing 'ordinary' women's bodies encourages readers to identify with them, and perhaps with the magazine as 'relating' to ordinary women. Juxtaposing the bodies of 'ordinary' women with homogenised images of 'model' women underlines the contrast between the two, arguably to the advantage of the magazine publishers.

In the context of *More* magazine, showing the naked bodies of 'ordinary' women, who are not models, functions in the same way as 'before and after make-over' features, where a photo is shown of an 'ordinary' woman 'before' and 'after' her transformation into a 'model' woman – with the use of beauty products and services. Within *More* magazine, the use of 'ordinary' women as subjects encourages the 'ordinary' reader to find fault with her own appearance, through comparison of body measurements, weight and age, and by identifying with those women who are not like the 'model' ('ideal') women in the magazine (McCracken, 1993). Presenting photographs of 'ordinary' women's bodies, in this context, supports a reading of those images through a discourse of self-improvement.

In sharp contradiction to *More*'s dominant theme of self-improvement, the 'Naked Truths' article and the editor's introduction addresses women within a discourse of self-acceptance. Self-acceptance can be achieved, not by emulating *More*'s homogenised images of 'model' women but by celebrating our *difference* from that 'ideal'. *More* tells readers that our bodies need improvement and at the same time tells us that we should accept our bodies because they are fine just as they are. This contradiction is managed by subsuming self-improvement and self-acceptance under a liberal humanist ethos of self-determination which masks, to some extent, the rhetoric of (illusory) free choice (Spitzack, 1990). The concept of free choice is illusory because it *does* matter which women 'choose'. In contemporary Western culture, both choices are not equivalent or equally available to women. The rhetoric of 'free choice' concerning women's physical appearance effaces the hegemonic power of normalising imagery (in this case the physical 'ideal' of femininity). The struggle between self-improvement and self-acceptance does not take place primarily at the level of ideology but at the level of material practice. Self-improvement means spending time, energy and money on managing and disciplining our bodies. These practices have normalising and disciplining effects because 'through the organisation and regulation of the time, space and movements of our daily lives, our bodies are trained, shaped, and impressed with the stamp of prevailing historical forms of selfhood, desire, masculinity and femininity' (Bordo, 1993a: 165–6).

The visual and verbal text of the magazine covertly and overtly support the self-improvement reading of the editorial. The rhetoric of free choice of self-determination decontextualises and depoliticises women's experiences. Inevitably, women's failure either to accept themselves or to emulate the ideal rests with the individual alone.

My readings are, of course, partial and temporary and among many possible readings. While the publishers try to anchor preferred meanings to the text, this is never wholly achievable because of the nature of discourse. There are always gaps, inconsistencies and the possibility of resisting dominant meanings. While I agree with the cultural critic John Fiske (1987), that we are not merely cultural dupes or passive consumers of culture, I would argue that it is erroneous to assume that alternative readings of popular women's magazines are readily available to the majority of women. Failure to acknowledge the power of normalizing imagery, in this case 'models', representing femininity as only white, young, thin, toned and flawless, renders women's experiences just as invisible as does the lack of acknowledgment of cultural and ethnic differences (Bordo, 1993a). It is not a straightforward matter, as *More* would have us believe, for women to assert the value of their 'difference' in the face of dominant social meanings (e.g. of 'beauty' and 'femininity') that reinforce feelings of inferiority and ugliness.

The reproduction of psychology's body image discourse, within popular women's magazines, is the focus of the next chapter. Through an analytic frame of practices of subjectification and using tools of discourse analysis, I examine further how women's bodies/subjectivities are regulated in the important empirical site of the popular magazine.

Notes

1. Circulation figures from the Audit Bureau of Circulations, Wellington, NZ, and from the Audit Bureau of Circulations, USA (website).
2. An earlier version of this paper was published in *SITES*, 'Radical Perspectives on Culture' (Blood, Spring, 1994).
3. Maori people are the indigenous people of Aotearoa (New Zealand).

5

PRACTICES OF SUBJECTIFICATION – 'BODY IMAGE' DISCOURSE IN POPULAR WOMEN'S MAGAZINES

Talk about body image in popular women's magazines marks a discursive shift in the way women's bodies/subjectivities have been problematised, and the subjectifying practices within which women are addressed and located. One of the earliest ways of problematising women's bodies/subjectivities within the context of women's magazines was via a discourse of 'body reduction'. Body reduction discourse produced women's bodies as 'excess' (see Spitzack, 1990). Dieting was presented as an acceptable and necessary feminine practice and a 'natural' life-long preoccupation for women. Common sense held that women wanted/needed to decrease their body size (a rhetoric of self-improvement) and that it was possible to do so. Women engaged in disciplinary practices, including monitoring of body weight, calorie counting and exercise to correct the 'problem' of excess weight.

Later discourses which problematised women's bodies/subjectivities included an anti-diet rhetoric, which emerged, ostensibly, in opposition to weight-loss discourse. Anti-diet articles became a regular feature in women's magazines and still appear today. Women were now castigated for dieting. Anti-diet discourse highlighted the harmful effects of dieting. Reducing caloric intake resulted in a slowed metabolic rate, leading to weight gain. Dieting could make you fat. Ironically, anti-diet articles and books (excerpts of which were published in women's magazines) almost uniformly began with a disclaimer about diets not working only to be followed by guidelines or regimes for 'healthy eating' (e.g. *Fit for Life*, by Harvey and Marilyn Diamond, 1985). The anti-diet approach gained the reputation, at least amongst critics, as 'the anti-diet diet' (Spitzack, 1990).

Publication of diets in women's magazines waned during the late 1980s and early 1990s. However, a discourse of body-reduction (e.g. 'look good – feel good' and 'slim equals healthy') remained an implicit – and often explicit – message in women's magazines (see Chapter 4 and below).

A recent and more powerful problematising discourse appearing in popular women's magazines is experimental psychology's body image discourse. Body image discourse marks a discursive shift from body reduction discourse and anti-diet rhetoric. Women's bodily 'excess' is not the problem. Rather, within a discourse of 'body image', seeing our bodies as 'excess' and wanting to reduce the size of our bodies becomes problematic – a sign of individual pathology. 'Body obsessions! Why we think we're fat' is the headline for *Cosmopolitan* magazine's September 1997 issue and the headline, 'the BIG issue – Why body image is a national obsession, why we're ruining our health to be thin, how to love your body, our cover girl Esme leads the way', sums up *New Woman* magazine's take on body image problems (April, 1997). Crucially, this discursive shift marks a change in the ways women are understood and how they understand and 'act upon themselves' – from being women with a problem of excess weight to women with a psychological problem of body image dissatisfaction and/or body image disturbance.

The first section of this chapter examines how, within body image discourse in popular women's magazines, women come to think of and act upon themselves as women with 'body image problems' (the examples of women's magazines were chosen as being representative or typical of magazines featuring body image articles). Second, I analyse body image articles featuring 'interviews' with hetero-sexual couples talking about the woman's body. I use an analytic vocabulary of interpretive repertoires and troubled/untroubled identities (Wetherell, 1998) to describe the patterns of meaning in the talk of these men and women and how these meanings produce women's bodies. Within a discourse of body image, embedded in the broader discursive field of popular women's magazines, women's concern with their bodies is read as a body image problem. The meanings men and women give to women's bodies and their explanations and justifications for women's concern about their physical appearance are highly contradictory. The effects of these contradictory patterns of meaning on women's bodies is discussed.

Practices of subjectification

I have already suggested that the question of how women come to think of and act upon themselves as women with 'body image problems' can be usefully approached by examining the practices of subjectification that produce women's experience within body image discourse, in the broader discursive context of popular women's magazines. Of central importance to my analysis is the linking of subjectifying practices with forms of power. As discussed in Chapter 3, power can be understood as productive and constitutive, working through, not against, subjectivity. In the analysis I take here, power does not simply constrain and dominate, but creates and forms people as subjects (Foucault, 1982). Power traverses all practices through which people are thought about, judged, helped, ruled, administered, and by means of which they come to see themselves and others as subjects of a particular kind (Rose, 1996: 25). In this view, subjectivity is not produced by experience but through the theoretically informed practices that produce experience (see Chapter 3).

Nikolas Rose, drawing on Foucault's writings on government and governmentality, uses the term 'government' to describe a perspective from which we can understand attempts by authorities (e.g. psychologists) to 'act upon the actions of others' in relation to certain objectives – of self-knowledge, self-realization, self-acceptance and so forth. Government emphasises how methods for 'the conduct of conduct' usually operate through attempts to shape the ways individuals 'experience, understand, judge and conduct themselves' (Rose, 1996: 29). Foucault referred to these strategies as 'technologies of the self' – techniques for the conduct of one's relation with oneself.

Foucault's writings on government and technologies of the self inspired Rose's formulation of directions for investigating practices of subjectification. His list of elements in the modes of subjectification include 'problematizations, technologies, authorities and teleologies', and provide a useful analytic guide to identifying the subjectifying practice, within body image discourse in popular women's magazines, which produce women as women with body image problems.

Problematisations

The ways human beings think, talk and act upon themselves have not emerged out of a reflection on the 'normal individual' or the 'normal personality'. Instead, the very concept of 'normality' has risen out of a concern and preoccupation with behaviour, thought and expression considered 'troublesome or dangerous' (Rose, 1996: 26). In understanding how we come to take ourselves to be persons of a certain kind, Rose argues we must look to the 'everyday practices' where behaviour has become problematic to oneself or others. In everyday practices and in the 'mundane texts and programs' (e.g. scientific discourse about body image that presents specific, named problems as facts, 'expert' advice and 'body image therapy' in popular women's magazines) 'problems' (such as 'body image dissatisfaction') are made visible, intelligible and manageable (Rose, 1996: 26).

Via popular magazines, a discourse of women's body image 'problems' is woven into the fabric of our everyday experience: 'The Bad News About Body Image: How many of us really like our bodies? The *Psychology Today* 1997 Body Image Survey, drawing on data collected over two decades, confirms that we are more dissatisfied than ever' (*New Woman*, April, 1997). Magazine survey results show that readers suffer from 'Body obsessions! The shocking results of our survey on food, fat and the female body . . . one in two women hate their bodies' (*Cosmopolitan*, September, 1997). Public confessions from 'real' women, about their bodily flaws, are a central feature of body image articles: 'I hate the fact that even when I lose weight my stomach and thighs are still flabby' (*New Weekly*, September, 1994). Body image problems are affecting our sexual relationships: 'Not tonight honey . . . I've got cellulite: how your body image affects your sex life' (*Cosmopolitan*, February, 1998).

Women (as in all women), we are told '. . . are more dissatisfied with our bodies than ever'. We 'distort our body size', and 'we have a distorted body ideal – what we think of as an ideal body is far too thin'. If we think that we have a good body image 'we are kidding ourselves' (*More*, 1994). 'One in two women hate their bodies', women 'suffer from body obsessions and think we are fat' (*Cosmopolitan*, September, 1997). 'Australian women are in the midst of a body image crisis' (*New Woman*, April, 1997). 'Our self-esteem is at risk' and 'We are at risk of developing eating disorders' (*Cosmopolitan*, September, 1997). 'We have a population of women who are unduly concerned about their weight and shape' while magazine survey results show that 'body dissatisfaction is universal among women in Western society' (*New Woman*, April, 1997). Women are told that 'True confidence means accepting – and loving – your body the way it is' (*She&More*, November, 1998).

Technologies

According to Rose (1996), *technologies* are the strategies that have been invented to govern the human being, to shape or form conduct in particular (desired) ways, embodying those desires in technical form. Rose argues that our very experience of ourselves as certain kinds of human beings (people of freedom, of personal powers, of self-realization and so on) is the result of a range of 'human technologies' that take ways of being human as their object. These technologies 'produce and enframe' humans as certain kinds of people (Rose, 1996: 26). Our lives are both enabled and governed within a technological field.

The pastoral relation

The 'pastoral relation' – a relationship of spiritual guidance between a figure of authority and each member of his/her flock (Rose, 1996: 26) – is the predominant human technology operating in body image discourse in women's magazines. Embodying techniques such as confession and self-disclosure, requiring self-inspection, self-suspicion, self-decipherment and self-nurturing, the pastoral relation is articulated in a range of different forms.

The pastoral relation of subjectification is articulated in the therapist–patient form between the omnipresent body image 'expert' and women (readers). For example, women are invited to assess their own body image problems with the 'body image test'. '*Cosmo* psychiatrist Dr Raj Persaud has devised this unique body image evaluator so you can find out how you see yourself, then discover the confidence-boosting tricks to make you really shine' (*Cosmopolitan*, January, 2004). Women are positioned in relation to the 'expert', within a discourse of body image, as needing advice and help with their body image problems. Psychologist Thomas Cash addresses women magazine readers as a concerned professional: '"Unlearn" negative feelings and behaviour. Every day look at yourself in a full-length mirror, both fully clothed and naked. But don't concentrate just on the parts you don't like (women with a negative body image tend to focus on their "faults")' (*Cosmopolitan*, January, 1998).

Self-scrutiny, confessions and public revelations of women's bodies/subjec-tivities are actively encouraged in body image articles. For example, 'Body Haters: Even supermodels . . . complain about their bodies. What's wrong with YOUR body?' asks *New Weekly* (September, 1994). The presentation of photographs of 'ordinary' women (sometimes naked), listing their bodily transgressions, has become increasingly common since the publication of the 'Naked Truths' article (see Chapter 4) in 1992. Similar articles include: 'Naked bottoms: ten women bare all' (*Cleo*, September, 1997), 'Which of these women likes her body?' (*NZ Woman's Weekly*, June, 1995), 'What I really think about my body: real women strip bare to share their most personal feelings' (*She&More*, February, 1998), 'Does size matter? Women talk about their body image' (*She&More*, November, 1998). 'Topless and bottomless – women talk about their lives' (*Cleo*, January, 1998). 'Love it, loathe it or just live with it. Real women rate their bodies' (*Marie Claire*, March, 2001).

In one genre of body image features, the 'couple' articles, women reveal/describe their bodies under the gaze of their male partners. The men, positioned as an authority, hear women's confessions and pass judgement on the women's bodies. This relation of subjectification is exemplified in the article: 'Men rate their girlfriends' bodies . . . the naked truth – Does your boyfriend think you'd look better with bigger breasts? Can you be sexy and flabby at the same time?' (*Cosmopolitan*, January, 1998). 'Couple' articles are the subject of my analysis in the final section of this chapter.

The magazine reader survey

The magazine reader survey is a central tool in the production of women as suffering from 'body image problems'. Surveys elicit knowledge about body image from readers via psychometric questionnaires similar to those published in *Psychology Today*. At the same time, magazines reproduce 'facts' about women's body image problems from other surveys. For example, *New Woman* (April, 1997) reproduced verbatim the report from the Body Image Survey originally published in the psychological journal *Psychology Today* (1996; see Chapter 1).

In the same issue of the magazine, *New Woman* (April, 1997) also published its own survey, 'Survey – Tell us what you think . . . *New Woman* wants to know your views on body image' – consisting of 10 questions with multiple-choice answers about women's feelings and beliefs about body size/shape, height and weight, dieting practices, levels of satisfaction/dissatisfaction with their weight as well as age, marital and employment status (*New Woman*, April, 1997).

The magazine survey is itself a discursive practice. It serves a rhetorical func-tion of presenting the 'truth' about body image in a persuasive, compelling and plausible manner. Surveys demand that women develop a relation to themselves of self-inspection and self-disclosure within the discursive frame of 'body image problems'. Simultaneously, other possibilities for making sense of women's experiences of embodiment are suppressed (e.g. women's anxiety about their bodies as the product of social power relations, rather than individual pathology).

An Australian publication of *Marie Claire* magazine (March, 2001) follows an article on body image with its own 'body image survey'. Telling readers that if they complete the survey, they will go into a draw to win $1000, the magazine addresses its readers: 'In the story, "How do you rate your body?", we asked women to discuss their shapes. How do you feel about your body? How would you rate your looks? *Marie Claire* is keen to know your thoughts' (March, 2001). Women are asked to think about 'your overall body image' and 'score your body on a scale from 1 to 10. A score of 1 would mean you have a negative body image while a score of 10 would mean you have a positive image' (March, 2001).

Magazine surveys are designed to elicit responses that frame women's experiences in a discourse of body image problems. For instance, *New Woman* Body Image Survey asks readers to answer: 'How satisfied are you with your weight?' and 'How do you describe your own body?'. Possible responses to the first question are limited to the degree of satisfaction/dissatisfaction women feel with their weight, and the latter question can only be answered from a range of responses from 'overweight' to 'underweight' (*New Woman*, April, 1997). Women's responses are 'read' as evidence of 'body image problems', therefore erasing or discounting real or potential alternatives.

The magazine reader survey is embedded in a text which provides readers with information about 'body image' – what it is, why we have 'body image' problems and how we can rectify these problems. Women are encouraged to learn about body image, to learn about themselves; for instance, 'Body image: how do you shape up?', asks Australian magazine *Marie Claire* (March, 1997). Women are positioned through these body image surveys and articles as 'naive' and in need of authoritative information and expert advice about body image. At the same time, presenting information about body image to women as something all women 'have', as something that can be identified and measured according to scientific 'norms' and as something women should know and be concerned about, encourages women to develop a relation of the 'educated' subject (of body image knowledge) to her self.

Body image discourse also encourages a particular relation of the self to the body. Because the concept of body image, (re)produced in women's magazines, is predicated on a fundamental split between mind and body (see earlier argument in Chapter 2), rectifying body image problems necessitates a particular relation of the self to the body. In order *not* to have a body image problem, women are encouraged to develop a particular relationship to their bodies – we must like our bodies, accept our bodies, nurture our bodies and, most importantly, learn to see our bodies 'as they really are' (see below).

Readers with 'body image problems' are addressed in the magazines by 'experts' in a therapist–patient relation. The 'therapist' is inevitably an 'expert' (most often a psychologist), a figure of 'authority', who is accorded the capacity to speak the truth about human beings and their problems. The psychologist/

therapist 'talks' to women/patients about their body image problems, offering corrective advice to help women change their thoughts and behaviours (which the 'experts' have identified as problematic). In this relation, women are subordinated to a therapeutic authority.

The majority of experts take the position of reassuring women about their 'normal' preoccupation with body weight and size. They also suggest that women should 'accept' their bodies, or at least change the negative ways they think about them. According to psychologist Judith Rodin, quoted in *Cleo* magazine:

> Many women feel silly about their preoccupation with appearance, eating and weight and think they should hide it if they want to be taken seriously. But those are not silly little complaints, they are personal and often painful concerns that deserve attention. All women share them to some extent. Whether we want to value, accept or change our bodies, we need first to change our minds.
>
> (*Cleo*, February, 1993)

Rodin reassures women that their preoccupation with 'appearance, eating and weight' is normal – 'all women share [it] to some extent' – that is, it is normal to have a body image problem.

Next Rodin offers us solutions to the problem. We, you and me, need to 'change our minds' and 'treat our bodies with respect'. This solution, formulated within a discourse of 'body image' problems, centres on change at the level of the individual. It is each woman reader who needs to change her mind (*Cleo*, February, 1993).

This emphasis on individual change is at the heart of Dr Thomas Cash's eight-step cognitive intervention programme for women called 'Private Body Talk'. Cash (see Chapter 1) advises women/patients to accept their bodies 'as they really are' (*New Woman*, January, 1997). In the introduction to Cash's work below, note the slippage between 'negative body image' and the even more pejorative term 'appearance obsession':

> 'Private Body Talk' is a term coined by psychologist Dr Tom Cash. Based on his studies of negative body image, Dr Cash developed an eight-step program to help people overcome appearance obsession. Private Body Talk is a big first step in helping you to accept who you really are'.
>
> (*New Woman*, January, 1997)

That Dr Cash is able to provide this '8-step plan' is due in large part to the separation of 'women with body image problems' from 'society' – he views these two as fundamentally separate and separable things. 'Challenge society's beliefs about beauty. You don't have to be a perfect size 10 to be loved, successful and happy'. An assumption that 'body image' problems and solutions lie in the information processing of individuals means that individual explanations are privileged over social/cultural ones. 'Learn to compliment yourself. Replace negative body talk with positive comments' (*New Woman*, January, 1997).

In the same article, Cash goes on to tell women '. . . discover what distresses you about your appearance' and 'practise getting comfortable with your body – relax and look in the mirror while focusing on your assets'. Using the word 'assets' in relation to women's bodies/subjectivities evokes sexualised images of particular body parts (large breasts, long legs, small waist) that will enable a woman to attract/keep a man. To speak of a woman's body in terms of 'assets' (re)produces women's bodies as commodities whose value in the marketplace depends on their 'quality' or, as the dominant message in women's magazines runs, on how we can best display and preserve them. Instructing women to scrutinise themselves in front of the mirror and focus on their 'assets' implies that women also have liabilities (excess body weight?) that must not be focused on. Cash encourages, under the guise of library practices, the very self-scrutiny he and his colleagues frame as pathological in women.

Authorities

Within popular women's magazines, women are not dominated or repressed by 'power', but are subjectified, educated and solicited by concerned professionals. The authority to speak 'truthfully' about women and women's body image problems is overwhelmingly accorded to psychologists. Psychological 'truths' and facts are characterised by the introduction and use of a language of body image, a set of norms, an assortment of technologies and a plethora of 'experts'. It is through the language and norms of body image discourse that women interpret and evaluate their experiences.

Prestigious researchers, authorised by their status as psychologists and/or university professors (e.g. Kevin Thompson and Thomas Cash – see Chapter 1) are introduced to readers as 'experts', able to describe, diagnose and offer solutions to women's body image problems. The extracts below (*Cleo*, February, 1993; *More*, April, 1994) are typical examples of the (re)production of the authority of academic research, and the establishment of the problem of body image in popular women's magazines. Judith Rodin, a North American psychologist, reports Kevin Thompson's research 'findings' as 'evidence' of 'body size distortion' (see Chapters 1 and 2 for an account of the original research). The rhetorical function of the heading establishes distortion of body size as a psychological problem affecting women. Thompson's status as an authority on women's body image is authorised by his position as 'a US associate professor of psychology'. Thompson's data supports a reading that 'body size distortion' is a problem (nearly) all women have. 'Body size distortion' exists, and is identifiable and measurable in individual women.

The language used here pathologises (nearly) all women – 'we distort our body size and lack a sense of our own shape and size'. 'Normal' women are invited to identify with the women tested who did not have an eating disorder, that is, other 'normal' women. The demarcation between 'normal' and 'deviant' is blurred because here 'normal' women suffer from 'body size distortion' just as women diagnosed with eating disorders do:

Why we distort our body size

Women often lack a sense of their own shape and size, which has a profound psychic outcome. If we are always pushing, reshaping and remaking our bodies, our sense of self can fluctuate too greatly, which is not psychologically healthy. Many women have problems figuring out how they look and feel – the physical component of their self-image is like quicksand.

Dr Kevin Thompson, a US associate professor of psychology, has tested women who were free of any symptoms of eating disorders. Participants were asked to estimate the size they judged their various body parts to be, using movable calipers. The psychologists then compared subjects' ratings with their actual measurements. More than 95% of the women over-estimated their body size, according to Dr Thompson. Their estimates were typically one-fourth larger than their bodies really were.

(*Cleo*, February, 1993)

This extract from *More* (April, 1994) also uses 'research findings' to make claims about the women's body image problems. The text below was super-imposed on a sketch of a magnifying glass, with the title 'Mirror, Mirror on the wall' in bold print, evoking an image of women as narcissistic and vain, overly concerned with their physical appearance.

'Body image' is introduced as something we all 'have'. The paternalistic tone of this piece exemplifies the relation between the authority (the researchers) and the (subordinate) women they address. The researchers know more about women's bodies/subjectivities than we do ourselves. Women do not know if they have 'a good body image'. We must rely on 'experts' to predict, diagnose and treat our body image problems.

If you think you have a good body image, you're probably kidding yourself, say British researchers. Studies show most women overestimate their body size and are unable to recognise their actual reflection in a mirror. Data from slim, healthy, 22 year-olds showed they overestimated their body size by 4.4% looking at it from the front and 3.7% from the side. Their ideal body image was about 5% less than their actual size. These women were deemed 'normal' in that they did not suffer from eating disorders or show any signs of psychological instability. The studies revealed the trend starts in girls as young as nine. By the time they are 14, they are significantly less satisfied.

(*More*, April, 1994)

Once again, the women who were 'unable to recognise their actual reflection in the mirror' were 'normal' – just like the magazine readers. Hence 'normal' women are pathologised.

As an authority on body image problems, psychologists tell women what their difficult experiences with food, eating and embodiment are 'really' about. A discourse of body image problematises behaviours (e.g. dieting) that were previously considered to be 'normal' and 'feminine'. The desire of (some) women to change the size and shape of their bodies is now indicative of individual pathology, that is, 'body image dissatisfaction'.

Psychological knowledge about women's bodies/subjectivities is presented, in popular women's magazines, as both expert and exhaustive. Women are produced as 'having' a body image that is (for most women) either 'negative' or 'distorted'. Body image 'actively influences our behaviour, self-esteem and psychopathology'. This suggests that psychopathology is something that individual women 'have' that lies dormant waiting to be activated. Girls' psyches are constituted as vulnerable and lacking: 'Girls harbour weight concerns and lack buffers to protect their psyches' (*New Woman*, January, 1997).

Teleologies

Another way we become subjectified as women with – or without – 'body image problems' is through Rose's fourth mode of subjectification, which is teleological in its form. Teleology is concerned with implicit aims or outcomes, the forms of life 'promised' by discursive concepts such as self-acceptance.

In order for women to come, ultimately, to accept themselves they need to understand their experiences (of being preoccupied and anxious about their appearance, eating and weight) as problems with their 'body image'. Their experiences must be rendered 'intelligible' to themselves (and others – the 'experts') through a psychological discourse of 'body image problems'. For this to happen it is necessary for women to come to understand themselves (within the pastoral relation and through techniques of confession, self-scrutiny and so on) in terms of their lack of satisfaction with their bodies.

Further, they must see the cause of their experiences of embodiment as the result of their own lack of self-acceptance and self-esteem. Confessing (to self or others) what the problem 'really is' – 'body image dissatisfaction' or 'body image distortion' – renders women amenable to regimes of expert advice and corrective treatments, such as Cash's cognitive intervention, 'Private Body Talk' (above).

The solutions offered to women for their 'body image problems' valorise an authentic, 'natural' body and self that women can strive to uncover through practices of self-acceptance, self-nurturing and cognitive change. This authentic self (the 'real' me) is accepting of her 'natural' body that is 'unique' and implicitly unmarked by social/cultural systems of meaning. This unproblematic celebration of diversity and uniqueness as 'natural' is captured in the heading of *She & More*'s article:

What I really think about my body – welcome to the real world, where women come curvy, lean, tall, short, big bottomed and small breasted – and have learned to love their shapes just as nature intended.

(*She & More*, February, 1998)

These 'psychologically healthy' women strive to resist societal messages that a slim body is the 'social norm'. They endeavour to free themselves from the constraints of unrealistic ideals of physical appearance. Their aim – the goal of these practices – is attainment of freedom from 'external influences' (the social), gained through admitting that they have a problem with 'body image', working to increase their self-esteem and to accept their body 'as it really is'.

Clearly body satisfaction (a rare commodity) offers relative immunity to media influence.

(*New Woman*, April, 1997)

'After body-image therapy, people can feel much better about themselves', says clinical psychologist and body-image expert Thomas Cash. Try these techniques.

(*Cosmopolitan*, February, 1998)

Regime of truth

Knowledge claims about women's body image problems constitute a 'regime of truth' about women's bodies (Foucault, 1980). Comprised of a series of statements that provide a particular way of talking about women's experiences of embodiment, body image discourse functions prescriptively to demarcate what can and cannot be said about women's bodies. This new discourse produces concepts and ideas about women's bodies which regulate and organise social practices in new ways – just as a body reduction discourse, discussed above, created a regime of truth which made practices of food restriction for women seem normal and obvious.

'Body image' discourse is presented in popular women's magazines as *the* explanation for (many) women's difficult experiences of embodiment. 'Body image' discourse serves a normalising function, classifying and categorising 'women' according to psychological 'norms' set by the discipline and offering corrective treatments to individual women. Psychological knowledge about women's 'body image' functions as an intellectual technology wherein body image problems are produced as individual pathology (we are dissatisfied with our bodies, we have distorted ideals, we are unduly worried and so on). Difficulties women experience with food, eating and embodiment are depoliticised and framed as a technical problem requiring (psychological) expertise to predict, diagnose and correct the problem.

'Men rate their girlfriends' bodies'

My focus on body image discourse in women's magazines turns to what I refer to as 'couple' articles. These articles are characterised by interviews with five or six heterosexual couples, usually accompanied by full-length photographs of the couple together, fully clothed – with the exception of a *Cleo* article, featuring photographs of naked women only and comments from male partners about the women's bodies (*Cleo*, January, 1998). In these articles, each 'real' woman and her (male) partner 'talks about' her body, specifically what each likes and dislikes about the woman's body. The material for this analysis is taken from the comments of the men and women interviewed in the following articles: 'Body image: how do you shape up? When it comes to the body it seems it's all in the mind. Jacqui Lang asks five women and their partners to describe what they see' (*Marie Claire*, March, 1997). 'Women with real thighs and the men who love them – these women all think there's something wrong with their bodies – but the men think they're fine. So who's right?' (*New Weekly*, May, 1997). 'Men rate their girlfriends' bodies . . . the naked truth: does your boyfriend think you'd look better with bigger breasts? Can you be sexy and flabby at the same time?' (*Cosmopolitan*, January, 1998). 'Love me, love my body – you've got to be a size 10 and look great to have a fantastic sex life, right? Not necessarily. Six women talk about their bodies and how they shape up between the sheets . . . and what their partners think' (*Cleo*, January, 1998).

When I first came across this 'new' genre of body image articles they struck me as bizarre and offensive. Women friends also expressed incredulity and distaste at the intimate and non-reciprocal revelations women made. The women's confessions were made *vis-à-vis* their male partners, who seemed to be potentially conferring (or witholding) patriarchal approval of women's bodies.

I was interested in the discursive function of these texts, that is, I wanted to understand what 'work' these articles were doing in the context of popular women's magazines and a discourse of body image. Specifically, I wanted to analyse how patterns of meaning in the talk of these men and women are worked through to produce women's bodies.

Before I move to this analysis, I first want to show how the magazine headers that introduce the articles, and the 'confessional' format of the interviews, constitute and enframe women's bodies as problematic or pathological. Magazine headers announcing 'couples' articles address the reader with a rhetoric of common sense about women's bodies. These pronouncements, introducing us to the women and men in the articles, echo the talk of experts about women's 'body image problems'. The dominant theme is, 'these women all think there's something wrong with their bodies' (*New Weekly*, May, 1997). These women are either mistaken in thinking there is something wrong with their bodies, 'when it comes to the body it's all in the mind' (*Marie Claire*, March, 1997), or, there is something 'wrong' with their bodies: 'Can you be sexy and flabby at the same time?' (*Cosmopolitan*, January, 1998); and 'Women with real thighs' – despite their 'real thighs', 'the men . . . love them' (*New Weekly*, May, 1997). These headings set up women's bodies as problematic – either because they are 'fine' but women believe there's something wrong with them (body image dissatisfaction?) or women's bodies are 'flabby' but their (male) partners still love them (so what are the women worried about?).

Confession, inevitably embedded in power relations, is a technique of the pastoral relation, the practice of subjectification at the heart of these 'couple' articles (see Rose, 1996, above). The women's confessions are striking for the very public, self-referential revelations they make under the gaze of their male partners. Almost without exception, women's confessions are an inventory of bodily flaws. Their disclosures evidence a rigorous self-scrutiny and self-knowledge that is a prerequisite for confession of bodily transgressions:

Tammy: I have no butt, my gut sticks out and I have huge thighs.

(*New Weekly*, May, 1997)

Danelle: I like my stomach because it's nice and flat. I don't like my bum and I feel really inadequate about my boobs.

(*Marie Claire*, March, 1997)

Nicolle: I've got long limbs and a short body. It's a bit out of proportion and I think I could probably lose a few kilos, especially round my middle area and especially as I get older.

(*Cosmopolitan*, January, 1998)

Rachel: I used to like how thin my body was, but I've let it get a bit out of control lately. I like my arms because they're quite thin and I also like the bottom of my legs. I don't mind my chest but I hate my stomach. It's the grossest thing about my body.

(*Cosmopolitan*, January, 1998)

Such confession does not simply tell the 'truth' about these women's bodies. The vocabularies, norms and systems of judgement, or ways women can 'know', understand and act upon themselves, are not provided by 'pure' introspection. Women come to relate to themselves 'as selves of a particular kind' in rendering that introspection in a specific vocabulary of feelings, beliefs, and desires and according to a particular explanatory system and authority (Rose, 1996: 32). Some of the women specifically use body image discourse:

Lee: When I was single my body image was definitely better.

(*New Weekly*, May, 1997)

Olive: My body image affects other parts of my life. There are things I don't do or haven't done because of my size – that goes for sex as well.

(*Cleo*, January, 1998)

The majority of the women describe their bodies as falling short of an implicit norm of physical appearance (see above).

How are the confessions of these women, exemplified in the extracts above, likely to be read by women in this context? There are at least two constructions operating here. Women, identifying their bodily flaws, are confessing to having a less than perfect body. The self-assessments of most of the women would fit neatly within a discourse of body reduction, where their confessions would be read as evidence of 'excess' body weight and/or undesirable body shape. Many of the comments women make about their bodies typify the statements that accompany photographs of women in the 'before' section of 'before and after' advertisements for weight loss services.

The 'coding' of women's experiences of embodiment as 'body image problems' comes not so much in the words of the women themselves, but in the contextualisation of those statements within the broader discursive frames set by the article and the men's contribution (see below). 'Confessing' women are produced as both transgressing the social norm for physical appearance ('I could probably lose a few kilos') and evidencing body image problems ('I hate my stomach, it's the grossest thing about my body'; *Cosmopolitan*, January, 1998).

Within a discourse of body image problems, women's confessions of bodily flaws and dislike of their bodies would be read as evidence of 'body image problems' – that is, as pathology. Normalisation of women's bodies occurs as a result of their confessions of deviance. Through a discourse of body image problems, women's confessions evidence that pathology is what is (most) 'normal' about women's bodies.

The confessional relation

Foucault has argued that confession is considered to be a libratory practice – it is valorised within Western society as the route to truth. Confession can be experienced as 'freeing' yet, as Foucault argues, confession is tied to practices of normalisation. Confession functions as a subjectifying practice which inevitably unfolds within a relation of power. The male partners of these women are not simply there to hear what the women say but are a source of authority in the confessional relation because:

> One does not confess without the presence (or virtual presence) of a partner who is not simply the interlocuter but the authority who requires the confession, prescribes and appreciates it and intervenes in order to judge, punish, forgive, console and reconcile.
>
> (Foucault, 1990: 61)

The men are positioned as arbiters of the women's bodies. They are photographed with their partners but their own bodies are not up for discussion. The men are authorised as more capable of giving an objective (authoritative) judgement about women's bodies, because they speak from the masculine, rational position. Men assume a pedagogic relation, offering advice to the (subordinate) women – who are illogical/irrational/mistaken about their bodies.

Further, men interviewed for the article 'Women with real thighs and the men who love them' are positioned as 'the men who love them'. It is men who 'make' women lovable. Here women are not lovable in their own eyes, but through the transformative gaze of men. It is 'the love of a good man' within a discourse of heterosexual desire that makes these women's bodies/subjectivities acceptable.

In these articles, men look at women's bodies, alternately judging, punishing, forgiving and consoling, for example:

> *Greg*: I wouldn't say Sondra's fat, but she has a big frame. Don't get me wrong, I think she's beautiful. She has nice legs, hips and thighs . . . She's may be 5 kg overweight, but not 10. Her stomach needs toning so I encourage her to work out.
>
> *(New Weekly*, May, 1997)

This relation of subjectification normalises men looking critically at women's bodies and produces the men's gaze as benign and caring, even nurturing. Relations of power are masked by this configuration.

Non-reciprocal visibility

Men's invisibility in a discourse of body image problems produces and maintains dominant gendered power relations. Women's bodies/subjectivities, focused on to the exclusion of men's, are produced through 'body image' discourse as pathological. The confessional ritual rules out his body as an object of scrutiny. The non-reciprocal nature of the confession within the broader discursive context naturalises women's 'body image problems' – and therefore the surveillance of women's bodies by others.

The man casts his judgemental, authoritative gaze over his partner, who does not gaze back. His body is not 'available' for scrutiny, neither does he offer it as such. Men represent 'normalcy' and the source of truth in relation to women who have 'body image' problems: '. . . these women all think something is wrong with their bodies' (*New Weekly*, May, 1997).

The magazine interview is presented as a 'vox pop' – as a straight sample of ordinary people who reflect common-sense views. But although the 'couple' interviews are presented as a veridical account of the men and women's talk, this is probably not the case. Journalists most likely interviewed a number of couples and selected those that responded in a way that supported the pre-selected story-line, that is, women think there's something wrong with their bodies, but men think women's bodies are fine. The 'interviews' would also have been heavily edited. This 'preparation' of the material shapes it to support a reading of women's talk as evidence of (widespread) 'body image problems'.

Discourse analysis – interpretive repertoires

To identify the patterns of meaning in this material, a more detailed form of discourse analysis is required than the descriptive form used in Chapter 4. In reading and re-reading the accounts given by the women and men, I looked for regular lines of argument in the way they talked about women's bodies. These discursive themes or 'interpretive repertoires', the key analytic concept used in discourse analysis, are the stories and narratives of 'identity' available in circulation in our culture. Interpretive repertoires are recognisable by particular statements, or tropes, which are usually internally consistent and bounded. These interpretive repertoires provide ways of understanding and giving meaning to experience by setting up subject positions. That is, people assume a particular sense of identity or subjectivity from different interpretive repertoires (see Chapter 3).

A central feature of people's accounts is their variability. A person might draw on different interpretive repertoires and move in and out of a number of different subject positions as he/she constructs his/her account. This means that people's accounts are often inconsistent and contradictory. It is this variability that is of interest to discourse analysts. By identifying interpretive repertoires, it is possible to see the patterns of sense-making possibilities which people can draw on at any given social/historical time.

To interrogate the magazine accounts which interest us here, from a feminist perspective, it is necessary to work both with the text and beyond it. This involves examining the text and then interpreting the significance of the discursive themes, organising the account in terms of their social meaning. The movement from talk to the interpretation of the place of this talk, the broader social context, is crucial in developing arguments about the political and ideological significance of particular kinds of talk (Wetherell, 1996).

From my reading of the magazine interview texts, I identified three central interpretive repertoires that structure the accounts. The women and men draw on these resources to talk about and describe their own or their partner's body, respectively. I outline these repertoires, providing instances of them from the texts in order to highlight the cultural assumptions about women's bodies in the text and look at how these interpretive repertoires work together to create an ideological field (Billig, 1987; Billig, Condor, Edwards, Gane, Middleton and Radley, 1988). This ideological field has to be negotiated, not just by the women in the magazines but by women in general.

The three main, clearly identifiable, interpretive repertoires used by the interviewees are: women's bodies as sexual objects of male desire; women as unnecessarily concerned about their physical appearance; and body work as essential to achieving and maintaining an attractive body.

Assuming these are actually the voices of real women and men, the types of responses expected from the interviewees are already anticipated in the lead-in to the articles. *New Weekly* magazine proclaims: 'Women with real thighs and the men who love them – these women all think something is wrong with their bodies, but the men think they're fine, so who's right?' (*New Weekly*, May, 1997). The question is rhetorical and appeals to common-sense understandings, both of women as critical of their bodies, and of men being able to look at women's bodies (more) objectively (see a similar line of argument used in the editor's introduction to the *More* article on 'body image' in Chapter 4).

Women's bodies as sexual objects of male desire

Women's compulsory visibility and the relative invisibility of men's bodies is writ large in 'couple' articles. One of the regular lines of argument in these accounts, drawn on by both men and women, produces women's bodies as sexual objects of male desire. Here desirable femininity is synonymous with a particular body shape (specifically, large breasts, long legs, small waist). 'Normal' and 'healthy' masculine heterosexuality is signalled by men's desire for (and implicit knowledge of) women's bodies and body parts:

> *Tony*: I don't like straight lines – I like a woman to be nice and curvy. I'm a bit of a butt man, so I must admit her backside does it for me more than anything else.
>
> (*Cosmopolitan*, January, 1998)

> *Glenn*: Her boobs were enormous when we met, which suited me fine. I'm a big-breast man.
>
> (*Marie Claire*, March, 1997)

> *Cliff*: She's just the sexiest thing on this earth. What little stomach she has I truly like. As Rosie O'Donnell once said, 'Bone is for the dog, meat is for the man'.
>
> (*New Weekly*, May, 1997)

> *Luke*: Nicolle has got breasts which is great and comes in at the waist which I love.
>
> (*Cosmopolitan*, January, 1998)

> *Pete*: If there's anything obvious lacking in Danelle it is probably breast size.
>
> (*Cosmopolitan*, January, 1998)

> *James*: I love the fact that she's buxom, really big up top, but her legs are nice and shapely.
>
> (*Marie Claire*, March, 1997)

Danelle: In intimate situations I think it would be a lot better for him if they [breasts] were a lot bigger because there'd be more for him to play with.

(Cosmopolitan, January, 1998)

Women as unnecessarily concerned about their bodies

Within patriarchal society, women are labelled the 'aesthetic' sex. It is women's bodies, not men's, that are gazed at and judged (see Bordo, 1993a, 1993b; Wolf, 1990). A woman's body is still considered to be more central to her 'identity' than a man's body is to his identity. An exaggerated importance is given to the physical appearance of women *vis-à-vis* men (see e.g. Malson, 1998). Women's prospects for relationships and intimacy (and increasingly, employment) are deemed largely dependent on their physical attractiveness to men (Bordo, 1993a; Wolf, 1990). In contemporary Western culture, women's bodies are 'up for' discussion, dissection and display.

A second interpretive repertoire used only by the men, in the magazine interviews, sets up the logic that women's concern with their physical appearance is unnecessary. This argument appeals to common sense about women's, supposedly inherent, narcissism. Even though it is unnecessary, women 'naturally' worry about how their bodies look. Some men argued that their partner's concern was unnecessary because they were not overweight. That is, women 'think they're overweight when they're not'. Many men accounted for their partner's concern about her physical appearance in terms of individual pathology. Women, men argued, were 'too self-conscious', 'exaggerating', 'unhealthy', 'insecure' and have a 'lack of self-esteem'.

Glenn: Although she (Charlotte) looks fantastic now she still keeps whingeing that she looks fat . . . she's lost a lot off her bum. She says it was huge but you know how women are.

(Marie Claire, March, 1997)

Cliff: It's hard to believe she's serious . . . no-one I know thinks she's overweight . . . the scary thing is she believes it about herself.

(New Weekly, May, 1997)

Greg: I wouldn't say Sondra's fat but she has a big frame . . . her big complaint is the size of her stomach – and I'd have to agree with her on that – although she exaggerates the problem.

(New Weekly, May, 1997)

Ted: I think it's unhealthy that she [Tammy] thinks she's overweight because she's not.

(New Weekly, May, 1997)

Luke: Like most women she probably goes on about losing weight. Most women go on about their thighs and Nicolle is no exception.

(*Marie Claire*, March, 1997)

Paul: When she whinges about her body I just tell her not to worry about it. Lack of self-esteem is her biggest problem . . . most women are insecure, let's face it.

(*Cleo*, January, 1998)

The discursive theme of women's-concern-as-unnecessary is employed by the men as they gaze at and judge (often critically) their partners' bodies as sexual objects. For example:

Luke: I've always liked her nice fleshy bottom and her hourglass figure. She does have short legs, quite muscular – I like them. Maybe her breasts could have been a bit larger and her legs a bit longer . . . But it's fine. I like her the way she is.

(*New Weekly*, May, 1997)

The contradictions in the men's views about women's bodies make it impossible for women to be 'unconcerned'.

Body work

The third interpretive repertoire that shapes the accounts of the women and men who 'speak' in women's magazines is 'body work', the argument that women's bodies require discipline. Disciplinary practices, including food restriction, exercise, self-surveillance and the exercise of will-power, were cited, by both men and women, as necessary and acceptable ways to achieve and maintain an attractive (acceptable) body. This repertoire sets up women's bodies as flawed and in need of remedial work, specifically body reduction.

Charlotte: Since I lost the weight he's [Glenn] been a lot more attracted to me, more touchy. He never told me to lose weight – but he was very encouraging once I started.

(*Marie Claire*, March, 1997)

Sondra: If I press him [Greg] really hard to tell me the truth, saying 'Don't you think I should go to the gym?', he'll tell me I'm right and that I should go to the gym.

(*New Weekly*, May, 1997)

Danelle: I get really paranoid about what Pete thinks of my body. I definitely think that since being with him I've been a lot more focused on my body. I just want to please him I guess. I never used to worry about weight but now I weigh myself three times a week.

(Cosmopolitan, January, 1998)

Pete: Body maintenance is a lifetime thing.

(Cosmopolitan, January, 1998)

Ted: Sometimes I'll say to Tammy, 'You need to get back in shape'.

(New Weekly, May, 1997)

Luke: I'd never force Nicolle to change her body shape. Sometimes I give her a stare across the table if she's going for her third piece of chocolate cake but that's a direct reflection of her wishes. When she's eyeing that third piece I say to her, 'Remember what you said about wanting to cut down on the amount you're eating'.

(Marie Claire, March, 1997)

A central element in this argument is that 'body work' is necessary because of the potential for women's bodies to 'get out of control'. For example:

Rachel: I used to like how thin my body was but I've let it get out of control lately.

(Cosmopolitan, January, 1998)

Linda: I do worry about my body – I think everyone does – I'm much more relaxed about my body image now than I was from my teens to my mid-20s. It's not that I've let myself go.

(Marie Claire, March 1997)

Luke: Sometimes she'll go on binges and eat heaps. I think that's a little bit silly. I ask her, 'Why are you eating so much?'. I'd never go so far as to tell her to lose weight; I don't need to. I have confidence enough in her to know that she wouldn't get overweight.

(Marie Claire, March, 1997)

The consistent and repeated theme of these 'couple' articles holds that women think there is something wrong with their bodies but their (male) partners think the women's bodies are fine. Men are positioned as the authority about women's bodies *vis-à-vis* women who confess their bodily transgressions. On the surface it seems that men are conferring patriarchal assurance, telling the women that their bodies are acceptable (and desirable) as they are.

As I have already indicated, a closer analysis of what these men and women are saying presents a more complicated picture. Here is an example of how these different interpretive repertoires of women's bodies as sexual objects of male desire, women as unnecessarily preoccupied with their appearance, and women's bodies as needing 'body work' to render them attractive (acceptable) are worked together in one man's account.

> *Glenn*: When I met Charlotte she was a bit plumper than now, but I had no dramas about that. She was fuller in the face and around the bum. But that didn't bother me. I like something to grab on to. Her boobs were enormous which was great! But although she looks fantastic now, she still keeps whingeing that she looks fat and I have to keep reassuring her, 'You look fine'. I do prefer her now. She has a really skinny waist. And her breasts are still a really good size. Charlotte doesn't have a perfect body, but I like it. She's definitely improved it heaps in the time I've known her. She's lost a lot off her bum. She says it was huge but you know how women are.
>
> (*Marie Claire*, March, 1997)

The interpretive repertoires identified in the talk of these men and women have a broader social significance, in that they both reflect and sustain current, dominant ways of talking about or giving meaning to (many) women's distress about their appearance, eating and body weight. These repertoires work together to constitute an ideological field, within which women are positioned, that is structured by certain dilemmas (Billig, 1987; Billig *et al.*, 1988). To confess to feeling unhappy and anxious about one's body is to be unnecessarily concerned with our physical appearance – a typically 'feminine' trait and, within a discourse of body image, likely to result in a diagnosis of 'body image dissatisfaction'. Yet, at the same time, women are expected to aspire to acceptable, desirable femininity, embodied in a physical 'ideal' to which 'ordinary' women bear little resemblance, if any. The discourse of body work speaks to the lack of any 'natural' beauty for women because their bodies require work to ensure their sexual attractiveness to men.

So how might this position the huge numbers of, especially young, women who are constituted through these discursive strategies? Women are presented with a paradox – on the one hand to be a woman, to be feminine and attractive (to men), requires a certain level of physical attractiveness against which 'real' women make comparisons. Here the spectre of the 'ideal' body hovers (evident on the pages of these magazines) as the epitome of feminine attractiveness against which 'real' women make comparisons. In contrast with this 'ideal' it is a straightforward matter to detail one's own physical shortcomings, indeed it is almost a requisite of normative (and normal) feminine behaviour.

In a culture that views women's bodies as commodities and the sexual objects of male desire, to dismiss women's concerns about their appearance as 'exaggerated' or 'unnecessary' reproduces the assumption that women are irrational and preserves the dominant representation of women's bodies as sexual objects by rendering that construction invisible. The workings of gendered power relations in maintaining women's bodies as sexual objects of male desire are effaced. The anxiety (many) women have about their bodies is (re)produced as a problem of individual women, not an effect or consequence of contemporary social organization and power relations.

The paradox of women's bodies as objects of male sexual desire *and* women as unnecessarily preoccupied with their bodies sets up a 'troubled identity' for women (Wetherell, 1998). Women know what the current standard is for femininity read as physical attractiveness. A discourse of self-improvement in relation to physical appearance is dominant in women's magazines, yet women's concerns about their physical appearance are dismissed here as trivial and unnecessary.

In summary, the psychological category of 'body image' popularised in women's magazines offers a discourse of individual pathology to account for (many) women's difficult experiences of eating and losing and gaining weight. Women are addressed and located in a therapeutic relation with a knowledgeable and concerned authority – psychology's body image 'experts'. In pursuit of self-knowledge and freedom from distressing experiences of female embodiment, women are exhorted to examine and decipher their experiences through a discourse of body image problems. The prize of freedom from 'body image dissatisfaction' is offered through a confession of bodily transgressions.

However, within a discourse of body image, women's confessions reveal deviance from 'normal' body image and are read as pathology. Normalisation of women's bodies takes place as a result of these revelations of deviance. Inevitably, these self-disclosures are heard as evidence that what is 'normal' is 'pathology'.

Constituting women as pathological, men stand, by comparison, in a position of health, of normalcy. Their own bodies remain invisible. Men, whether the partners of women or the scientific experts, are positioned as arbiters of women's bodies. The discourse of body image reproduces gendered power relations.

The next chapter is based on an analysis of one woman's talk about her experiences within the context of a conversation we had together about 'body image'. Using the concepts of discourse analysis, subject positions and interpretive repertoires, I explore how assumptions of experimental body image research constitute her subjectivity in particular ways, and discuss the effects of this constitution.

6

BODY IMAGE TALK – ONE WOMAN'S ACCOUNT OF HER EXPERIENCES

A 2 hour conversation I had with Emma, a 31 year-old woman, about 'body image' forms the basis for the following analysis. Emma and I have a casual friendship of 3 years' duration and we meet perhaps half a dozen times a year. Emma offered to talk to me about her own experiences for my research (which in the early days I still referred to as 'body image research').

In previous chapters I have explored the discursive constitution of women's bodies/subjectivities in different sites: within experimental psychology's body image discourse, within one particular article in a popular women's magazine featuring 'ordinary' women naked, and in the (re)production of psychology's body image discourse in popular women's magazines.

I have suggested that scientific, experimental research assumptions about body image contribute to women's everyday understandings about their bodies, specifically their experiences of physical appearance. A discourse analysis of one woman's (Emma's) account of her everyday experiences of embodiment is the focus of this chapter. I examine how the assumptions of body image research and their effects in women's bodies are exemplified in Emma's talk, which, I argue, underlines the ways women in mainstream Western culture can understand their embodiment.

Analytic concepts and approach

The text below comprises extracts of my conversation with Emma. My role in this conversation was 'researcher', but not the 'objective' researcher of scientific psychology. My aim was that this 'interview' would simply be a slightly more formal – and recorded – version of similar, everyday conversations women have with one other. Our conversation was transcribed in full and provides a rich account of one woman's experiences of being 'overweight' – weighing more than what is considered 'the norm' by current Western standards.

Discourse analysts treat discourse as a potent, action-oriented, medium of meaning-making. My analysis is based on the idea that subjectivity is constituted or constructed through the discursive meanings available to women and men at any socio-historical moment. Discourses provide subject positions, which constitute our subjectivities in particular ways. My aim is to explore how Emma constructs an account of her self using the discursive resources of 'body image'. I take a discourse analytic approach to examine the flow of discourse in Emma's account, that is, 'the formation and negotiation of psychological states, identities and interactional and intersubjective events' (Wetherell, 1998). This means paying close attention to the way in which Emma constructively describes events that, for her, imply particular causal accounts, as well as looking at the social/cultural patterns and resources available for her to do this. Discursive resources available to Emma to talk about her body include assumptions (re)produced in body image discourse in experimental psychology and popular women's magazines. The potential social and political effects of these particular discursive patternings are also a focus of this analysis.

The view of subjectivity not as something one 'has', as in traditional psychological notions of 'having' a personality, but rather as something one 'does', opens up theoretical possibilities for exploring the changing as well as contradictory nature of people's accounts. I am interested in the variability of the complex constructions and practices Emma 'does' in constructing herself. I take tasks of constructing a self as highly context/interaction-specific, designed to bring off or 'accomplish' certain discursive acts, such as the blaming of others, blaming of self, and so on (Edwards and Potter, 1992).

Interpretive repertoires and subject positions

People's accounts of events and reasons they give for their actions are variable. Accounts are characterised by inconsistency – people often give more than one version of events and, as the communication situation changes, so does this version change. Such variation most often occurs between relatively internally consistent and bounded discursive themes or interpretive repertoires (Potter and Wetherell, 1987; see also Chapters 3 and 5).

The contradictory subject positions that Emma moves in and out of, and the different interpretive repertoires that set these up, are crucial features of Emma's account. The concept of 'subject position' originated in Althusser's (1971) notion of ideology as 'hailing', 'addressing' or 'interpellating' the individual, producing her as a unified subject (the one who is addressed), named by ideology. The subject positions in Emma's account are inevitably linked to the broader sociocultural or ideological context and its interpretive repertoires which 'hail' her – providing Emma with ways of giving meaning to her experiences.

The interpretive repertoires that resource Emma's account set up subject positions, sometimes in opposition to each other (i.e. a negative or a positive position). The interpretive repertoires or discursive themes take up recognisable and bounded lines of arguments, that is, claims and statements (Wetherell, 1996). I identify interpretive repertoires used by Emma, locate them within the broader social context, and consider the significance of these particular organisations of meaning for women.

Assumptions (re)produced within experimental psychology's body image research (see Chapter 1) are identifiable discursive themes or interpretive repertoires resourcing Emma's account and offering subject positions or possibilities for constituting subjectivity. One of these assumptions is the mind–body split.

Objectification of 'the body' – the mind–body split

The assumption that the body is a separate object from the mind, which underpins experimental psychology's body image discourse, is a striking feature of Emma's talk. Body image research and Emma's talk both (re)produce a woman's body as an inanimate object. In this formulation the body is viewed as an object, separate and separable from the mind that perceives it.

Emma takes up the position of an objective 'I', able to view her body as an object at a number of different points in her account. One of the reasons that I had wanted to interview Emma was her description, in an earlier conversation we had, of what I saw as 'a shift' in the way she viewed and experienced herself. In the space of recounting an incident at her workplace, Emma moved from talking positively about herself and 'being-in-her-body' and not focussing on her physical appearance, to seeing her body as the object of her gaze in a very negative way. I was interested in exploring what this 'shift' was about and how to make sense of it. From conversations with other women and my own observations, this sort of movement in the way women view themselves is a common feature of women's talk. The following extract, taken from the first few minutes of my conversation with Emma, is Emma's account of this experience. The extract illustrates this 'shift' from 'being-in-her body' to seeing her body as an object.

Sylvia: When you gave a description of giving a training seminar in your job I imagined you being really competent, organised, doing it spot on, really professional, etc. I can't remember if you said what the feedback had been like but I got the impression that it had gone really well and it was polished. Then when you described seeing the video of the training session . . .

Emma: Ohhh, horrific . . .

Sylvia: Your focus on how your body looked to the exclusion of anything to do with your performance. And when I think about body image/self-image that was such a clear example . . .

Emma: Yeah . . . it was. And it is a tragedy because I am so able [crying] you know. I know I am incredibly capable and all I could see was this big fat blob [crying]. And it's a shame because in a way it's this whole, almost the grief thing about being angry, this grief that I lose everything else and I am angry, at me because I lose looking at the lesson in that

108

case . . . who I am and the purpose of that whole thing to the stupid obses-sion about how stupid I look. I can give you another very good example of this.

We had a karaoke evening about 3 weeks ago and it was organised at work and I was feeling in a bit of a rebellious mood before I went out so I got dressed up in my favourite clothes which is this black swing jacket but it is really big and its got big buttons down the front. In summer I wear it with leggings and flat shoes but that night I wore black tights, my Doc Martens. I was in a real tough guy, this is what I am like when I am not at work mood, it was almost extreme. With this pleated chiffon skirt underneath it you know, so it was a really short skirt and this amazing fabulous hat I've got with beautiful material flowers. I just felt really good in it and a bit off beat and a bit of a tearaway and it is absolutely not my work image which is you know suit and a jacket and sensible shoes. So we turned up and I had the hat on and I look great in hats and I just love hats and I was completely into it from the minute we got there. All I wanted to do was get up and sing a song on the karaoke machine and, in fact, I was the first person up there to sing a song with a woman whom I work with who's got a fantastic voice and I felt completely alive, like it was amazing we got the harmony right and the power in the singing and just loved it. And the whole night, I was the one who was doing most of the singing and I'd get everyone else up to do the singing and we sung 'These boots are made for walking'. It was just fantastic, I really enjoyed it and Trisha who we lived with, her jaw dropped she just couldn't believe that this was the same person she lived with because I was so much in there and onto it. Well I had a fabulous time, really enjoyed it. Anyway we got back to work and they had taken lots of photos and I just looked at the photos and thought 'My God, you look ridiculous' you know? [crying] I'd had such a great time and I saw that photo and all I could see were these fat podgy legs. [crying] It wasn't how I imagined them, I didn't feel like I saw that I looked in that photo and all I could see was 'Oh that looks, you know, stupid'. Then I compared my fat podgy black legs to all the other legs and, you know, I couldn't even fit into those jeans. I'd enjoyed it so much and then I saw the photos and thought 'Don't be silly Emma' and I said 'Oh I look terrible' and other people said 'No you don't' so I sort of looked at the body from the head up and I thought 'Yeah, well you do look quite good and I looked like I was enjoying it and I've gone back and had another look' and it has not got so bad the third and fourth time. Ohhhh [deep sigh] but again you know I had had such a fabulous time and I had felt . . . and I'll probably never wear that blimmin' skirt again because the legs look so podgy and how I am after that is different because of the way that I see I looked in those photos. I won't wear that same outfit again and even the hat I've got two thoughts about now and it is a fabulous hat and I like hats.

In Emma's reading of and response to the images, in both the video and the photographs, she is positioned in a way which creates a dramatic alteration in her self-conception. There is a shift from Emma positioning herself as '*I am*' to positioning herself as '*all I could see*'. She takes up the subject position of spectator of the spectacle of her body. This is evidenced in her grammatical shift from first person, '*I*', to the third person, '*You look ridiculous*' and '*All I could see were these fat podgy legs*' and '*so I sort of looked at the face*'. Her body becomes the object of her (critical) gaze.

At a later point in our conversation, Emma gives another description of her body as object:

Emma: While there are things about me that sometimes I don't like generally I think I like my approach to life and I like the friends that I have and the values I've got and then there's this body that I don't like. The arguments I put forward I quite like and my sense of ease about things I like. I don't actually take anything too seriously. I'm not into great order, I'm not pedantic and I've got this body that I don't like [crying]. Sometimes I'm too sharp with people and sometimes I don't keep my word and I'm sorry about that, but it's not an innate problem you know it's overcomeable but the body somehow it has happened and it's not the ideal.

Body image discourse does produce Emma's mind–body split, as exemplified in her talk, but also psychological research on body image holds that women with 'body image problems' are saturated with dissatisfaction with their bodies. There is no room for contradictory thoughts, feelings, behaviours or desires. When it comes to body image dissatisfaction, women either have it or they do not (see Chapters 1 and 2). Yet women do not *always* feel dissatisfaction with their bodies and often experience their bodies positively as well as negatively, despite there being no change in the size or shape of their bodies. What is striking in many women's talk is the contradictory nature of 'women's bodies' – the simultaneity of opposite perceptions.

It is clear from Emma's account that seeing herself as the object of her own gaze is not her only experience. Emma begins her account from the subject position 'I', the generalised human 'I'. This 'I' is metonymically linked to her body. We can see from the position Emma takes up in describing her performance in the training session, 'I am incredibly capable', that this 'I' is the rational 'I', imbued with the ability to see clearly and objectively. This 'I' also serves as a narrative device which functions to provide the impression of consistency and unity amongst the different subject positions.

Emma also uses the referent 'I' as the subject position of her rebellious self. The language she uses in this construction, 'I was in a real tough guy, this is what I am like when I am not at work mood . . . it was almost extreme' and her account of the experiences of her rebellious self (lines 2–12) suggests the positive value Emma gives this identity. This is an 'I' that Emma constructs quite differently and differentiates from the 'I' who is 'incredibly capable' in the paragraph above by her self-positioning as 'rebellious, a bit of a tearaway', 'it is absolutely not my work image', and 'Trisha who we lived with, her jaw dropped, she just couldn't believe that this was the same person she lived with because I was so much in there and onto it'.

Later in our conversation Emma describes her experience of embodiment in yet another way.

Emma: I had a really nice pair of shorts, they fitted really well and I actually felt great all summer. I was still a bit podgy and overweight but they fitted, they weren't tight and they looked quite good and I felt really good in them. I had a real sense of freedom and literally lightness and joy in a funny sort of way in terms of relating to my body you know. I felt much more comfortable with it and it was almost like we were more of a whole person than we are now, where I usually feel quite like, this isn't it . . . you know. I see it's a surprise that we've become almost separate [crying].

Here Emma talks about her body/self as 'we'. There is a simultaneous sense of fragmentation and fusion/engagement with her body, rather than simply her seeing her body as an object of her gaze.

Seeing my body 'as it really is'

A second assumption of body image research exemplified in Emma's account is that it is possible, indeed 'normal', for women to view our bodies accurately and consistently over time. This assumption evokes the concept of a 'real' body or one 'truth' about the body that can be perceived. It also demands a consistent 'self' – the authentic or true self who is able to accurately perceive the body 'as it really is'.

In Emma's account the task of seeing her body 'as it really is' is complex. At times she privileges the photographs of herself and the video image (and her reading of them) as 'true' because she can 'objectively evaluate' her body, that is, see it 'as it really is'.

Emma: It is there in black and white, and I can compare it to other people in the photo or my vision of what other people look like on video. It's a person that I can sort of evaluate compared to other people, and that's a fat person. Like I am able to objectively evaluate almost, if I can see it on the video – well that's the video Emma, there's no tricking that. And in the photographs I can look at it like it's someone else.

Emma's desire to be objective and know the truth about her body, to see it 'as it really is' with 'no tricking' causes her confusion and distress as she attempts to determine whether the 'fat blob' or the 'rebellious self' is her 'true' identity.

Emma: All I could see were these fat podgy legs [crying]. It wasn't how I imagined them. I didn't feel like I saw that I looked in that photo.

The contradiction for Emma between how she feels (her experience at the party) and what she sees (in the photographs) is highly problematic for her. Does she privilege, with the status of truth, how she remembers feeling at the party or how she sees she looks in the photographs? In terms of an identity, this creates the dilemma, who am I? Am I 'incredibly capable', or 'a bit of a tearaway, a real tough guy', or am I a 'fat blob'? The subject position Emma occupied at the party, or her 'identity' there ('You know I was completely onto it from the minute we got there and I felt completely alive and it was just fantastic I really enjoyed it') is brought into question, becomes precarious, when she sees the photographs. The assumption that it is possible and 'normal' to see one's body 'objectively' and consistently over time forces Emma into a distressing position of having to know the truth about who she 'really' is. At this point in her account, Emma argues that the video and photographic images reveal the 'real' Emma – the subject position of 'fat-blob'. Her identity becomes like the photographic image, fixed and static, rather than a multiple and shifting subjectivity evidenced in her account above and below.

Her distress and confusion as to which 'body' is the authentic Emma is compounded because in contemporary Western culture a social norm of physical appearance operates as a standard of acceptable femininity/sexuality for women. In her account Emma describes herself as being 'outside' of what is normal in terms of physical appearance, so to accept her 'objective' view of her body is to see herself as 'not normal', that is, not feminine. I return to this point later in this chapter.

It is important to remember that talk is always embodied, that is, discourse has material effects. Emma's subject position at the party, 'rebel' and 'off-beat', is a more precarious identity as a result of her experiences of viewing the photographs. One of the effects of having to 'see her body as it really is' (at this point in Emma's account as 'fat blob') means that Emma will alter her behaviour in future.

Emma: How I am after that is different because of the way that I see I looked in those photos. Like I won't wear that same outfit again and even the hat I've got two thoughts about now. From a body image point of view I think each time I see myself like that it actually makes a difference to how I behave in the world the next time. I wouldn't wear the same things and the equilibrium goes down a bit, I feel the seesaw is on the downside. I don't perhaps feel as confident.

The view of the body as asocial, which underpins body image research, is evidenced in Emma's account in her search for the 'truth' about her body. There is no room in this perspective for Emma to comfortably hold opposite perceptions of her body simultaneously, to see her body as produced through socio-historical

112

discourses about women, sexuality and the female body. The search for the 'authentic' body and the need to know the 'truth' about herself is a central focus of Emma's account.

Accepting one's body as it really is

A theme related to the notion of an authentic body that can be objectively perceived is that women must accept their bodies 'as they are'. Within a discourse of body image, being critical and/or dissatisfied with one's physical appearance is understood as indicative of pathology, that is, body image dissatisfaction. In Emma's account, her distress about her body presents her with another dilemma. She sees herself as a 'fat blob', yet at the same time is aware that it is not all right to express this concern with her appearance:

Emma: I lose looking at the . . . purpose of that whole thing [the training seminar] to the stupid obsession about how stupid I look.

In this statement Emma is simultaneously positioned as both critical of her appearance and also, given this negative description of her body and/or her emotional response to seeing herself in this way, as 'stupid'. Within a discourse of body image, a negative focus on physical appearance is regarded as pathological. This is carried into women's everyday understandings of their bodies. Women's preoccupation with appearance is considered to be unnecessary, unhealthy, exaggerated and not justified. Body image research and advice in popular women's magazines tell women they should accept their bodies as they are (see e.g. Chapter 5). This presents a contradiction for Emma between the distress she feels because she perceives she looks like a 'fat blob' and her rendering her distress as unreasonable or 'stupid'.

The individual vs. society

The bifurcation of society and individual underpinning body image research results in individualistic explanations for women's anxiety and distress about their bodies. The cause of 'body image dissatisfaction/distortion' is located in the minds of individual women. 'Society' is an external variable that can influence women's 'body image' (media representations of 'ideals' of feminine beauty; the message that thin = sexy, and so on), but it is the responsibility of individual women to resist societal influences. In her account Emma reproduces this birfurcation as two issues:

Emma: There are two issues, one is a societal one and one is a personal one. And on the societal level there are very clear things that women are supposed to be and I recognise that I am not that. I'm not even in the running for attractiveness, socially I don't think. On an individual level, I'm the only one that I hurt by worrying about it. I mean it's me that's imposing,

I suppose you could say society is setting up the norm but I'm the one that is actually making me suffer by it and it's my own interpretation as to what is appropriate that pours me back into my bottle.

I know all this is made up but I'm the only one that sort of imposes. I'm the one that says ultimately, 'They think you're stupid', which is just an invention that I've made up, you know I've somehow decided that this isn't OK.

Emma views her distressing experiences centred on body size through a repertoire of individualism. In terms of formulating a sense of identity, she sets up an account which places the responsibility for her distress firmly in her own hands, 'I'm the one that is actually making me suffer'. She positions herself as the autonomous, rational, individual who, pitted against society, should be able to resist the 'made-up-ness' of societal pressures on women to conform to a particular body size. In this formulation, societal pressures become 'just an invention I've made up'.

This positioning causes further distress for Emma because, on the one hand, a repertoire of individualism means that she should be a strong individual able to ignore societal pressures but, on the other hand, Emma experiences the very real effects of social norms that operate to discipline women's bodies. At this point in Emma's account her body becomes 'it' or 'this':

Emma: I mean it gets in the way of being OK. I do a good job. I am very able, I am fun and inspiring and then stupid old me gets upset because I realise that I look, well I feel that I look stupid and it gets in the way. I am angry that somehow I have this vision that this is not all right. I am a human being and this is my one chance [crying] at it, this is it, this is life and I am spending it not doing things because for some reason I sort of don't think this is acceptable.

Emma describes her experiences of shopping for a shirt and being confronted with what she describes as 'clear evidence' about what is considered to be normal in terms of body size for women in contemporary Western society. This evidence is seen as irrefutable, and certainly not 'just an invention' of Emma's.

Emma: Someone, I don't know who, has decided that a size 14, and I reckon that's a small size 14, you know, is as big as people get. Well that's an absolute black and white, I mean it's not even at my own suggestion. It's clear evidence that people aren't bigger than a size 14. I mean if you are bigger then there's something terribly wrong with you or if you're bigger than a 'Large' my God what's wrong?

Emma is contradictorily positioned as a 'fat blob', unacceptably large according to current social norms, and simultaneously as an autonomous, rational individual who can (and should) see past the 'made-up-ness' of social norms. This means that, while the social norm of a rigid standard of acceptable physical appearance for women shapes and defines Emma's experiences of female embodiment, she blames herself for her distress – 'I'm the one that is actually making me suffer'.

Self-surveillance and the social norm

Knowledge claims made by body image researchers delimit the questions that can be legitimately asked about the anxiety many women feel about their bodies. Crucially the individualistic repertoire effaces the thoroughly social nature of subjectivity, through a fundamental separation of the individual and society. The powerful, productive effects of social/discursive practices in constituting and regulating women's experiences are rendered invisible.

On the view that subjectivity is discursively constituted, dominant discourses of patriarchal society constitute women's bodies/subjectivities (our desires, thoughts, behaviours, ways of understanding the world) in particular ways. For example, women's bodies, particularly in popular media, are produced as objects of male sexual desire and as needing remedial work to render them acceptable. At the same time, women's concern with their physical appearance is unnecessary, unhealthy, and trivialised as a 'feminine' preoccupation. These ways of thinking and acting upon ourselves shape our experiences in particular ways (see Chapter 5).

One of the central, and most powerful, interpretive repertoires shaping Emma's subjectivity in her account is the 'social norm', the idea that a woman is defined by her appearance in terms of a norm of physical appearance. 'Normal' appearance for women is represented by a historical and cultural 'ideal' that is, in the contemporary West at least, young, thin, taut, toned and white. Homogenised images of 'ideal' femininity/(hetero)sexuality have powerful normalising effects for women (see Chapter 4). In her account, Emma explains the reason for her (very evident) distress about not fitting 'the norm' as something she does to herself.

In contrast, from a Foucauldian perspective, the operation of a norm (in this case an 'ideal' of physical appearance for women) is at the heart of surveillance. The 'social norm' for physical appearance requires of women self-surveillance and self-regulation to that norm (see Bordo, 1993a, 1993b). Our desires to be thin, attractive and sexually desirable and the meanings of these desires (happiness, approval, acceptance, heterosexual romance/bliss and so on) are powerfully shaped by a norm of physical appearance for women. Our bodies are normalised and disciplined in relation to an 'ideal' of physical appearance/femininity (see Chapter 3).

The effects of the 'social norm' of physical appearance are exemplified in Emma's account above, and more explicitly below. Emma constructs her subjectivity (or sense of self) in relation to this norm of physical appearance. The effects of this norm include self-surveillance and self-regulation. In this extract from Emma's account she is explaining her distress on seeing the photographs of herself following the karaoke party:

115

Emma: It was black and white. It was a visual image like an image you see in magazines. Like in terms of when you see photos of people or still images of people, this is not what is OK. And I see myself as someone nice and acceptable and if I look at, nice and acceptable and middle of the road and appealing and attractive and someone you would want to be a friend with, if I just looked in the broad term of images, that is not [emphasis] the image.

One of the things I noticed about Emma's responses to the video and the photographs was her surprise at the images – this is evidenced in her comments, '*all I could see were these fat podgy legs* [crying] *it wasn't how I imagined them. I didn't feel like I saw that I looked in that photo*', and '*All I could see were these terribly chubby legs. It was an unexpected shock*'.

Sylvia: You talked about seeing the photos as being a shock.
Emma: It was a stunning surprise . . .
Sylvia: It made me wonder, what would you have expected to have seen?
Emma: More my . . . something more normal . . .
Sylvia: And by normal you mean . . .?
Emma: Thinner legs, like not the chubby . . . look you can even see it here if I pull these up [pulling up her skirt to show me her legs]. My knee, the knee's a bulge and then it goes straight, there's a bulge below my knee (laughs) you know . . . and that's not what, attractive people I suppose, successful, attractive people who are . . . [sigh] you know . . . if we had a drafting race and we were drafting people for . . . almost being in a movie about being in society I suppose, you know I would be drafted out into the dud pen . . . [crying] because there is a bulge in the wrong place.

Not being 'normal'

Emma's self-surveillance, examining her body, showing me where it deviates from what is normal, is an effect of a socially imposed norm. Emma evokes the idea of what is 'normal' (the social norm of physical appearance for women) as a standard against which she determines her own acceptability. Emma's account evidences the self-regulating function of the social norm – she scrutinises her body, she knows the norm that operates and its standard for physical appearance and she envisions the gaze of others directed at her own 'deviant' body.

Emma's illustration of the normalising power of an 'ideal' of physical appearance is sobering. 'Drafting' is a powerful metaphor of selection (and exclusion) based on an established norm predicated on a visual criterion – one look is all that is required to make a decision that she is a 'dud' and to 'draft her out'. The drafting metaphor conveys the power of common sense, a highly regulated and rigid social norm of physical attractiveness in constituting and regulating Emma's body/ subjectivity (or sense of self).

116

An obvious feature of Emma's account of her experiences is that 'fat' is a devalued subject position – to be fat is problematic. For Emma, being fat is equated with being 'not normal', 'not acceptable' 'not okay' and 'not appealing and attractive . . . someone you would want to be a friend with'. When Emma sees herself as a 'fat blob' she is unable to simultaneously accept that her 'rebellious self' is one and the same person. Being fat rules out certain emotional experiences – when Emma saw the photographs of herself after the party, it contradicted her experiences of being 'out there, and onto it' at the party.

In terms of formulating a sense of identity, one of the central interpretive repertoires resourcing this account is the personological repertoire (Wetherell, 1996). This repertoire sets up mutually exclusive subject positions, where fat is the negative or devalued position and thin the positive, valued subject position. Personality characteristics are conflated with body size. Because of the either/or construction of these subject positions, there is no subject position for women to feel and behave as Emma did at the party *and* to look the way that Emma perceived she looked in the photos. Emma privileges the visual authority of the photographs, and takes up the negative subject position. Emma explains and justifies her self-positioning after seeing the photos as 'This is a person that other people would notice as being not acceptable'.

Within the personological repertoire it is not just being fat that is a problem, but fat means being unacceptable. The negative and devalued subject position (fat) contained within the personological repertoire is reinforced, in the following extract, through its opposition to the positive subject position of thin – the socially endorsed subject position.

Emma: I suppose what I want to be is a free spirit, you know, lightness, joy, vibrance, aliveness, and what I see is someone who is verging on . . . I've still got that thing about this teacher who told me I'd be a big-busted Women's Division of Federated Farmers matron, you know standing up there in my tweed suit and I don't want . . . I don't identify with that . . . I don't want to be an old conservative woman I want to be a free child really, you know an adult but fun and a dag[1] you know and a free spirit and to make other people laugh and have a good time and . . .

Sylvia: Like you were at the karaoke . . .

Emma: Exactly! And that was the loss really that what I saw, it looked more like . . . ohhh not the person who would do cartwheels on the beach . . . you know someone who would sit under the umbrella.

Emma's desire is to be a free spirit – a free child, light, vibrant, joyful. Emma's 'free spirit' implies the promise of freedom from the problems of embodiment. Emma describes, in her account, a solution to her distress through transcendence of the corporeal.

Despite Emma's account of her experience at the karaoke party as one where she was her 'free spirit' self (evidenced by her response to my comment above),

117

Emma's awareness of the operation of a social norm for women's appearance means that when she sees her body as not the ideal of femininity (lightness, joy, vibrant, a free child), she re-evaluates her remembered experiences. This re-evaluation is made in light of what she sees as the 'truth' about her body – that it is a 'fat blob' – and her view of herself as not 'normal' (i.e. feminine, acceptable) limits the possibilities of who she can be and what she can experience.

Emma's account is rich in the cultural assumptions available to Western women for making sense of their experiences of feeling/being overweight, and feeling anxious about the size/shape of our bodies. Her account exemplifies key assumptions that underpin body image research. Assumptions of a mind–body split that encourage objectification of the body, a view of 'normal' body image as an accurate and consistent perception of one's body over time, the belief that it is possible and 'normal' to see one's body 'as it really is' – these assumptions are predicated on a fundamental split between individual and society, where the body is 'natural' and not a social product. The effects of these assumptions, it must be noted, are interactive, not simply a one-way process.

Emma's account also evidences the multiple, contradictory and shifting nature of subjectivity. Emma constructs her account of herself both in terms of body image research assumptions and against these assumptions. Her experiences at times are constructed against the cultural thrust of body as object, closer to Orbach's (1978, 1988) notion of the body as owned and lived in. Her perception of her body shifts over time and there is evidence of the simultaneity of opposite perceptions of her body. Her attempts to uncover her 'true' identity or see her body 'as it really is' create confusion for her and she explains her self-positioning as 'fat blob' with recourse to individual vs. society explanations. Emma is critical of social norms of physical appearance and refers to their arbitrary or 'made-up' nature at the same time as she perceives her subjectivity (or sense of self) as determined or disciplined by these norms.

Emma is able to render critical readings of central assumptions that shape and limit her experience. She constructs her subjectivity by drawing on a range of available discursive themes. The variability of her account and the contradictory nature of her subjectivity introduce the possibilities of political choice between different modes of femininity in different contexts and between the discourses in which these have their meaning (Weedon, 1987).

Within experimental psychology's body image discourse, such possibilities for women are erased. Within a discourse of body image problems, the anxiety and distress (many) women experience about their bodies is read as individual pathology. Ignoring the social (by reducing it to a variable) and rendering the body knowable only as an object of perception, body image research forms a self-fulfilling, self-perpetuating cycle. Having discovered 'body image dissatisfaction' and 'body image dysfunction' as psychologically 'real', women's talk about their distress about their bodies is seen as evidence of these problems.

Inevitably, and unfortunately at the expense of women, body image research simply describes its own (pessimistic and pathologising) production.

In the final chapter, I examine the clinical implications of the arguments presented in this book.

Note

1. "Dag" is a New Zealand colloquialism for a fun person.

7

CLINICAL IMPLICATIONS –
FROM THEORY TO CLINICAL
PRACTICE

What are the clinical implications of the arguments outlined in this book? We have seen how the assumptions that form the basis of body image research, including its mind–body dualism, perceptualism, realism and the society–individual dichotomy, lead to the pathologising of individual women whose experience of their bodies causes them distress. I believe a view of women's embodiment and subjectivity, as discursively constituted, and an understanding of the material effects of different discursive constructions enables alternative, and arguably more useful, approaches to working with women.

How can these alternative theories of the self/body/world inform our clinical practice? What is the relationship between women's eating difficulties and their concerns about physical appearance, a relationship formulated in body image research as simply causal, where unhappiness with physical appearance is seen as the *raison d'etre* for women's eating difficulties? Who are the women struggling with a dislike of their bodies if not the unitary, rational–irrational, subject(s) of body image research? How can women have different, positive experiences of our bodies and eating? How might we learn to experience our bodies differently, and not just as objects of our critical gaze? How can we understand and help women to usefully explore the relationship between their eating and their experiences of embodiment?

This chapter attempts to answer some of those questions. Drawing on similar themes in the works of a diverse group of clinicians and academics, I look at ways that women's distress and anxiety about their bodies and food might usefully be approached. In presenting a social constructionist approach, I am putting forward a particular epistemological view that is only one of a number of diverse ways of working with women with eating difficulties. The approach presented here is not intended to be prescriptive or a step-by-step guide to clinical practice and I refer the reader to the works referenced in this chapter, which include outlines of clinical interventions.

There are significant differences amongst women who seek help because of their distress about their bodies and their eating difficulties. Clearly there are differences in working clinically with women whose well-being is compromised by a low body weight, and who struggle to manage their day-to-day lives, and working with women whose anxiety and distress about eating and body size has not had such a dramatic impact on their day-to-day functioning. Therapy must be tailored to the needs of individual women. However, to insist on a distinction between women with an 'an eating disorder' and women who experience distress about eating and their bodies but do not meet the criteria for a diagnosable 'eating disorder' medicalises eating difficulties and masks how *commonplace* women's experiences of inadequacy, shame and self-hatred are (Bordo, 1993b).

Attending to the clinical implications of the arguments outlined in this book means highlighting a social and systemic approach to thinking about women's difficulties with food and their bodies. Introducing these still somewhat margin-alized ideas (see e.g. Orbach, 1978, 2002) into an area of psychology dominated by positivist assumptions and interventions opens up possibilities for more fruitful ways of making sense of women's experiences.

In the 1970s and 1980s, Orbach (1978, 1986) and other feminist psychother-apists made a significant contribution to the way that women's difficulties with their bodies and food could be thought about (see e.g. Dana, 1987; Dana and Lawrence, 1988; Lawrence, 1984, 1987). Similar themes in the work of Chernin (1983, 1985), Garrett (1998), Hirschmann and Munter (1995), Knapp (2003) and Becky Thompson (1994) emphasise a social analysis of these difficulties. Roth (1983, 1986, 1996) and Boskind-White (2000) are among those who have contributed to understandings of the complexities of women's relationships with their bodies and food. There are, of course, theoretical differences amongst this diverse group, but most of these writers take a social constructionist view where language, meaning, subjectivity and the body are thoroughly social (see Chapters 2 and 3). Implicitly and explicitly, they detail a social and political (feminist) analysis of women's experiences and avoid practices that classify, pathologise or blame individual women for their distress.

In this view there are good reasons why women develop difficulties with food. Discourses of race, gender, class and religion constitute women's subjectivities/ bodies in ways that have a profound impact on our ability to feel at home in our bodies, to experience them as 'lived in' rather than as 'always imperfect' objects. Turning to food as an attempt to deal with trauma is a common coping mechanism for women. Childhood trauma, including emotional, physical and sexual abuse, has been implicated in the eating difficulties many women experience in their adult lives (Thomson, 1994). The reason a child or an adolescent may begin using food to deal with unbearable situations may be different from the reason she continues to use food as an adult.

Many women restrict their food intake or binge and purge in an attempt to deal with distressing emotions and/or intolerable circumstances. For women, their bodies are often the repository for their negative feelings. Girls and women turn to food – overeating, self-starving, purging or a combination of all three – in an attempt to manage painful and overwhelming feelings. However, the attempted 'solution' then becomes the problem. In order to change these ways of using food, it can be transformative for women to learn to eat in response to physiological signals of hunger and to stop eating when satisfied. In terms of hunger and appetite and knowing what, when and how they like to eat, women make these discoveries themselves.[1]

The constitutive nature of language

Working from a social constructionist approach marks an epistemological shift from experimental psychology. This means remaining alert to the constitutive force of language and how language is used to communicate meaning in culture. When a woman says that she is dissatisfied with her body, that if only she wasn't so 'fat' everything would be okay, her talk is not seen as reflecting the 'truth' or 'reality' about her body. The focus is on how a woman's language is used to communicate meaning. Women often speak about their distress in terms of 'feeling fat', 'needing to lose weight' and 'if I was thin I'd feel more confident'. It is important to recognise that the words 'fat', 'thin' and 'overweight' are not just physically descriptive and that we need to explore what it means for individual women to see themselves in this way (Orbach, 1988). This means that a woman may use the word 'fat' to express how she feels about her body, irrespective of body size. For example, a young girl who is not eating might attribute her distress to her 'fat' body, saying her body is 'stink'. Over time she may come to recognise that she, herself – some sense of embodied self – feels 'stink', that she experiences her life as 'stink' and it is not only (or even) her 'fat' body that is the source of her unhappiness.

When we listen and talk with women about their distressing experiences with food and their bodies, how we talk constitutes those experiences and has material effects on the lives of individual women. For example, some women say that their difficulties with food mean they are 'crazy' or 'greedy' or they 'have no self control'. For example, Nadia had been eating and purging for a number of years and was very controlled in other areas of her life. She described how she felt when she binged and purged. She would ensure the house was empty and she had plenty of food in. She felt safe knowing she would be alone all evening and not be interrupted. When she got home, shutting the door behind her, anticipating being able to eat and purge without interruption, she said she felt 'real freedom'. Nadia surprised herself that she should feel this way, when previously she had only been aware of feeling out of control and terribly ashamed about her eating and vomiting. She was then able to begin to explore why she felt bingeing and purging was the only way she experienced 'real freedom' and how she might allow herself to experience freedom in other ways.

Bulimia was referred to by one woman as her 'best friend' and another said she was frightened I would take bulimia away from her – she was fearful because overeating and vomiting felt to her like the only way she had to cope with life. It is important to attend to the way women make sense of their own difficulties and to the ways that language constitutes a particular reality for each woman. Attention to the meanings of food, eating and body size is crucial if we are to usefully explore why women use food in the way that they do and how these eating practices may be serving individual women.

Food, eating and embodiment

It is not possible to talk in any meaningful way about working with women who feel unhappy with their bodies without acknowledging the connection between women's experiences of their bodies and their eating patterns. While many women who feel dissatisfaction with their bodies may not seek professional help, most women who experience sufficient anxiety about the size and shape of their bodies would likely have attempted to control their body weight in some way, through either food restriction, bingeing and purging or excessive exercise.

Working clinically with women who are distressed about their body size and shape means working with women who have difficulties with eating. When a woman experiences distress or anxiety about her body, this is most often expressed through her relationship with food. How, when, what and why a woman eats is inextricably tied to her feelings about her body.

Becky Thompson (1994) argues that the traumatic basis of some women's eating problems teaches us something about bodies and embodiment, because trauma often disrupts an intact sense of our bodies. Bingeing, dieting and purging, she suggests, are emblematic of 'a rupturing of women's embodiment', where women's ability to be grounded in and connected to their bodies is interrupted. How a woman feels about her body affects the decisions she makes around food. For example, if a woman who feels she is 'fat' binges, she may then berate herself and begin to restrict her food intake. Alternatively, she may feel a sense of failure and hopelessness and continue to binge, 'punishing' herself for her lack of control by eating until she is uncomfortably full. Women often interpret their difficulties with food as the cause of their unhappiness with their (unsatisfactory) bodies. They believe that if only they ate less they would be thinner, they would like their bodies and they would be happy.

Despite a strong desire to lose weight and a fear of gaining weight, women frequently commence therapy saying they are exhausted by their preoccupation with food and often frightened by it as well. They long to be free of what many describe as their 'obsession' with food.

Concern about physical appearance

Within body image research, body image is narrowly defined as solely a physical appearance-related construct. Not surprisingly, then, body image researchers have 'found' that women's distressing experiences of their bodies are caused by their concern about physical appearance. It is well established that there are many reasons why women develop difficulties in feeding themselves and why we feel uncomfortable in our bodies. The work of Orbach (1978) and others (see e.g. Hirschmann and Munter, 1988, 1995; Roth, 1983, 1986) articulates the problematic role of food in the lives of many women and the way in which the language of food and the body is used to communicate emotional distress. Thompson argues:

> Identifying the traumatic bases of many eating problems reveals the dangers of labelling a common way women cope with pain as an appearance-based disorder. One blatant example of sexism is the notion that women's foremost worries are about their appearance, a belittling stereotype that masks women's worries about paying the bills, keeping their children off the streets and in school and building loving and egalitarian relationships. By highlighting the emphasis on slenderness, the dominant imagery about eating problems falls into the same trap of assuming that difficulties with eating reflect women's 'obsession' with appearance. This misnaming fails to account for the often creative and ingenious ways that girls and women cope with multiple hardships, quite frequently with no-one's help but their own.
>
> (Thompson, 1994: 8–9)

These more complex, social understandings of women's difficulties with food and their bodies are effaced by the insistence of body image discourse that women's difficulties are caused by their own, self-generated, irrational concern about their physical appearance.

Meanings of body size for individual women

There is no simple causal relationship between eating difficulties and a concern about physical appearance. Investigating the meanings of body size with individual women, it is possible to explore what leads a woman to see herself as 'fat' and view her body as the cause of her pain. It must be acknowledged that women often experience anxiety if they feel their bodies do not approximate the current Western ideal of feminine beauty. A woman's unhappiness and painful feelings – for example, feeling inadequate or ineffective in her daily life – frequently centre on her (imperfect) body, fuelling her desire to achieve or maintain a thin body.

At the same time as we explore the meanings of different body sizes with individual women, we need to be aware that changing eating patterns will almost always be reflected in changes in a woman's body size and shape and these changes will have particular effects for individual women. For example, women who have maintained an artificially low body weight by restricting their food intake are often fearful they will gain weight if they eat when they are hungry. It is crucial to address this with women, looking at the meanings individual women attribute to weight gain and living in a larger body. When women with a history of dieting and binge-eating begin to eat in response to physiological hunger signals and stop when full, they often lose weight (Hirschmann and Munter, 2000; Orbach, 1978, 1988). For many of these women, their experience of living in a smaller body does not match their fantasies about what their lives would be like when they were 'thin'. Many women become aware of problematic aspects of a smaller body size. Maria, who had binged and vomited for a number of years, reported losing a great deal of weight through a national weight loss organization. She had bought a new dress and went to her end of year office Christmas party looking very different to previous years. Maria said she got a great deal of attention, particularly from male colleagues, and many comments about her body and how good she looked. Maria noticed that she was feeling increasingly upset during the party. She left early and drove home via a takeaway restaurant. She stocked up with food, went home, ate it all and vomited. It was only after some time that Maria realised that she had felt angry at the party; 'Just because I lost weight, people wanted to know me. But I was still the same person I had been before. I'd been to that party for 4 years in a row and no-one paid any attention to me before'. Problems with food are not simply related to concerns about physical appearance. It is important to be alert to fluctuations in weight because of the meanings – conscious and unconscious – individual women attribute to their bodies and how they make sense of their experiences at different body sizes.

From body as object to embodiment

Within body image research, a woman's body is viewed as an object and 'body image' is conceptualised as a quantifiable psychological construct. In their quest for the truth about women's bodies, body image researchers uncritically utilise the dominant forms of knowledge in Western society, those that are informed by counting, weighing and measuring (Garrett, 1998). This is evident in their claims to be able to accurately measure a woman's experience of her body by getting her to estimate the width of her 'body parts' – her hips, thighs, chest and face – to ascertain her level of 'body image dissatisfaction'. An alternative approach to knowing and experiencing one's body emphasises the cultivation of 'inner' bodily awareness. Developing an awareness of feeling states and physiological states is crucial in learning to 'live in' or fully inhabit one's body.

In working with women with difficulties with food and embodiment, the aim is to help women to move away from viewing their body as an object that can be moulded and shaped and to move towards experiencing their bodies as lived in. One of the key features of this work is to explore the meanings and emotional states women attribute to different body sizes. A rhetoric of 'change your body, change your life' dominates weight-loss discourse. Thinness, in early twenty-first century Western culture, is synonymous with success, femininity, sexuality and control over oneself and one's life. Not surprisingly, many women hold onto the belief that if only they were thin their lives would be great. Many women I work with equate thinness with a pain-free existence, believing that if only they were thin they would transcend the pain they experience in their lives at present. Being thin is seen as the panacea for everything, from relationship problems to financial difficulties. Given the dominant meanings of 'thin' for women in our culture, many are reluctant to give up the hope that 7 lbs or 2 stones are all that stands between them and happiness. Many women continue to speak about their unhappiness and dissatisfaction in the language of food and the body:

> In a country brimming with images of youth, whiteness, thinness and wealth, it makes painful sense that dissatisfaction with appearance often serves as a stand-in for topics that are still invisible. In fact, it is hard to imagine what the world might be like if people were able to talk about trauma and the ways they cope with it with the same ease as they talk about dissatisfaction with their weight and appearance.
>
> (Thompson, 1994: 11)

Thompson is talking here about America, but her comments about the dominance of 'youth, whiteness, thinness and wealth' are applicable to much of the Western world. It is a common experience for women to view their bodies as objects in need of improvement. Improvement usually means making our bodies – but not our breasts – smaller and firming and toning our bodies. Given the cultural thrust of the body as a malleable commodity that can be made to emulate the ideal of feminine beauty, it is no surprise that women are rewarded for approximating the cultural ideal. Viewing our bodies as invested with meanings, desire and an unconscious enables women to explore the meanings and fantasies they hold about their bodies at their current 'fat' or 'overweight' size and to explore fantasies they hold about what their lives will be like once they are thin.

'Fat' and 'thin' fantasies

A useful way to break down the 'objective' stance women view their bodies from is to use guided fantasies. These fantasies, or guided visualisations, are a rich source of hidden and often contradictory meanings women hold about body size and the emotional states they attribute to different body sizes (see Hirschmann and Munter, 1995; Orbach, 1978, 1982; Roth, 1989). For example, when Sue imagined herself thin, she saw herself lying on the beach wearing a bikini. When asked how she had felt being thin in her fantasy, she said, 'I was just lying there being thin!' Her fantasy of being thin was synonymous with having 'arrived', but this gave way to Sue feeling 'like a store mannequin, not a "real" woman'. When 'thin', Sue also experienced herself as passive and inert, which contrasted with her fantasies about the vivacious, sexual woman she would be once she was thin. It was new information for Sue to realise that some aspects of being thin were not as positive as she had fantasised. An 'objective' approach to body size and shape is more complex when we look at the meanings individual women attribute to 'the thin body'.

Women's fantasies of being their 'ideal' (thin) body size often reveal aspects of themselves that they do not feel able to express at their current body size. For example, Meg, a young woman who weighed more than the cultural norm, said that if only she were thinner she would be free to get up and dance on the bar with her friends when they went to the local pub at the weekend. She felt because she was 'fat' she would be laughed at and was monitoring her behaviour to avoid humiliation. When Meg lost weight, she said she realised she did not want to dance on the bar, because 'it just isn't me, it isn't really something I'd feel comfortable doing'. Meg felt this way despite the fact that she was more comfortable with her body size and shape than she had been previously. She now chose not to dance on the bar because it made her feel uncomfortable, not because her body was not acceptable enough – thin enough – to display publicly. It is often a surprise for women to learn that they have internalised other cultural norms that influence the way they conduct themselves, regardless of the actual size of their bodies. Many women experience this 'inner' knowledge as freeing, seeing it as something 'personal' and particular to who they are. This represents a shift from feeling that it is their unacceptable bodies that dictate what they can and cannot do.

Women can begin to 'own' their own bodies through the use of fantasy work. Sue, who imagined herself lying on the beach 'being thin', began to realise that she did not like feeling her body to be on display, like a mannequin. Meg, in deciding she did not want to dance on the bar – regardless of her body size – was not splitting off her body as the flawed aspect of herself, stopping her from having fun. Instead she experienced herself as having personal boundaries that precluded her doing something she was not comfortable with. Another woman, Chloe, went on a hike with a good male friend. It was a hot day and when they reached the beach, they wanted to swim. As neither had swimwear they decided to swim naked. Chloe said she had always believed that when she was thin she would not feel constrained about displaying her body. However, her experience of being a smaller body size was quite different. She kept some of her clothes on, not because she didn't feel good about her body, but because she felt more comfortable in the presence of her friend keeping her clothes on. This was a shift for her from fantasies about display and openness that she had previously felt shut out from because of her unacceptable body. She learnt that she had 'internal' constraints – feelings about what felt comfortable to her – that were an important part of her embodied experience that meant she did not want to expose her body in that situation.

The 'real' me

The idea of a true self or 'the real me' inform women's fantasies about who they will be when 'thin'. The old adage, 'within every fat person is a thin person waiting to get out', typifies this thinking and is particularly compelling for women who, understandably, wish to conform to the cultural ideal of beauty. When women are exposed to ways of talking and thinking about themselves and their experiences, that attend to the shifting and changing nature of subjectivity, they can begin to see that there is no one 'true self' or 'real me'. Women often become curious about how they feel in different social situations and with different people. They begin to notice that their behaviour is characterised by variety and inconsistency, and to accept this without censoring their behaviours as they might have previously. They begin to 'extend their repertoire' of who they are beyond the usually available mind–body distinction. Women begin to see that there is no 'body' that can be objectively and accurately perceived, that their experience of their bodies is informed by how they feel at given times. Significantly, women's experience of their bodies shifts from viewing their body as an object to be moulded or shaped to an appreciation of embodied experience.

Spirituality

For some women, developing a spiritual aspect to their lives has been central in shifting the way they view and experience their bodies. For example, Buddhism has provided some women with an alternative understanding of their bodies – not as the cut-off, flawed aspect of themselves, but as integral to who they are, to be respected and cherished. This view has enabled them to experience themselves as embodied and to bring a compassionate awareness to the way they see their bodies and how they feed themselves. A practice of mindfulness has helped some women to become more attentive and responsive to cues of hunger and satisfaction. Meditation has been very useful in enabling some women to experience their bodies differently, again as 'lived in', not as a separate object (see e.g. Albers, 2003).

Embodied eating

Women's difficulties with food and eating are imbricated in their experiences of embodiment. Many women's relationship with food is so fraught that they either restrict their food intake, binge following food deprivation or overeat as a prophylactic measure before the new diet starts on Monday. Many women would not see their eating in these terms, describing it instead as a lack of will-power, inability to stick to a diet or because they love food. However, even women who protest that they overeat because they love food do not seem to take pleasure in their eating, since eating is frequently followed by feelings of guilt and self-flagellation and, of course, critical appraisal of the over-fed and 'fat' body.

The most significant change women can make to interrupt this cycle of restriction followed by bingeing and purging is to stop dieting (Hirschmann and Munter, 2000; Polivy and Herman, 1987). Dieting leads to bingeing, which leads to self-hate, which leads back to over-eating. Dieting, bingeing and purging, we come to distrust both our bodies and our appetites. Women's fear of weight gain is actively promoted by the billion-dollar weight-loss industry. Our fear of our appetites and of losing control around food keeps many women locked into a diet–binge cycle. When women do lose weight through dieting, they are still not able to relax and 'eat normally' for fear of regaining the weight. Rates of recidivism following weight loss are around the 98% mark – women's anxieties about regaining weight after dieting are certainly well-founded.

The fact that dieting leads to bingeing and weight gain was one of the corner-stones of Susie Orbach's (1978) work *Fat Is A Feminist Issue*. Orbach claimed that if women learn to eat when hungry and stop eating when satisfied they will reach an 'organic' body weight and their weight will not fluctuate dramatically – as it does when dieting and bingeing. Losing and gaining significant amounts of weight interferes with a woman's ability to 'know' and feel grounded in her body. Many women have a 'fat' and a 'thin' wardrobe and vacillate between at least two body sizes. Women say when they are 'fat', that it doesn't count because they are trying to get 'thin' and when 'thin' they report being anxious lest they get 'fat' again. The experience of regular and often significant weight fluctuations makes it impossible for a woman to come to 'know' her body.

The political and gendered nature of women's painful experiences of food and the body, foregrounded by Orbach's (1978) work, has largely been negated. The radical nature of her ideas has been 'watered down' for popular consumption and harnessed to dominant ideas about food restriction and self-control. For example, in Orbach's book, eating when not hungry is viewed as an issue to be explored, as it would yield valuable understandings about a woman's hunger and how this might be satisfied without eating if she is not hungry. It is now common-sense knowledge that women eat when stressed or bored or in need of comfort. Tips about how to avoid eating for comfort run alongside articles about 'healthy eating' and diets. In her book *Fight Fat after Forty* (2000), Dr Pamela Peeke promises to teach women 'How to stop being a stress eater and lose weight fast'. Within a discourse of body reduction, eating for comfort or because we are under stress is reframed as simply another stumbling block to successful dieting and long-term weight loss.

Deciding not to restrict their food can free women to acknowledge the emotional, physical and financial costs incurred in dieting. Dieting is experienced by many women as, inevitably, self-punishing, infantilising and humiliating (Blood, 1996). When women decide not to diet again they are often relieved to know they will not deprive themselves of food any longer (Hirschmann and Munter, 2000; Orbach, 1978, 1988). They do not want to return to the disciplinary and self-monitoring dietary practices that previously shaped and dominated their lives. In stopping dieting, women also frequently report a fear of losing control of their eating and gaining weight. This happens because, for many women, their only experiences of eating since childhood have been food restriction and bingeing (ibid).

It is a subversive act to refuse to restrict and monitor our food intake because we fear our appetites and bodies are 'unacceptable'. It has been argued that 'recovery' from eating difficulties is the 'real rebellion against docile bodies' (Garrett, 1998: 190). To stop dieting is to take back the authority of external sources – weight loss organizations, partners, family members – and learn to trust our bodies and our appetites.

Women who have either restricted their food intake and/or binged for many years need to re-learn how to eat when they are hungry and stop when satisfied. Ignoring hunger pains, overriding physical feelings of fullness, or feeling unable to tolerate fullness and then vomiting have usually characterised these women's previous experiences of their appetites and bodies. Many women are accustomed to eating in response to other feelings, such as sadness or distress. They frequently eat in response to external cues, such as a diet sheet or when their partner or children want to eat. This can mean that they are completely out of touch with their own physiological signals of hunger and satisfaction. When women learn how to recognise their physiological signals of hunger, to eat in response to them and to eat foods they enjoy and feel hungry for, the relationship a woman has with her body can change significantly (Hirschmann and Munter, 2000; Roth, 1983, 1986, 1996).

When women start to eat when hungry and stop when satisfied they begin to experience their bodies as a source – and an increasingly reliable source – of knowledge about their appetites and needs. As women learn to eat in tune with their hunger, they experience both physiological and psychological satisfaction, which increases their confidence in their ability to feed themselves with care (see e.g. Hirschmann and Munter, 2000). Women's talk about their bodies changes; they are less likely and less able to talk about their bodies as an 'it' because their experience of their bodies has shifted. When women feel hunger, respond to it and feel satisfied they have the experience of 'living in' their bodies. This appears to be a dramatic shift for women who have previously felt dissociated from their bodies.

As well as learning about their physiological signals, women begin to discern feelings of hunger from other feelings that may have led them to eat when they were not hungry (Orbach, 2002). For example, for some women anxiety or loneliness are interpreted as hunger and this leads them to eat. As well as learning how to eat when their bodies need food, women also learn that their feelings are embodied and an integral part of who they are. Building on their new experiences of their bodies as shifting and contradictory, women can learn to discern different feelings, and learn how to bear these rather than eat in response to them. This process breaks down the mind–body dualism. Women begin to have a new confidence and trust in their appetites and their ability to satisfy them.

Meanings of food, eating and embodiment

As women become more conscious of a range of bodily experiences, they notice that how they feel 'in' and about their bodies is in constant flux and is very much contextual. It may not seem a great revelation to report that women say they begin to notice how their experience of their bodies is contradictory, shifting from moment to moment, particularly in different social situations. However, an understanding of women's experience of our bodies as shifting and contradictory is very different from experimental psychology's insistence on 'normal' body image as a 'consistent and stable' construct. As women are encouraged to adopt a stance of curiosity about how they experience their bodies, they become aware of a range of embodied experiences – sadness, anxiety, pleasure, tiredness. In the past women have tended to respond to uncomfortable feelings by eating, or not eating, or bingeing and purging. They begin to attend to different aspects of their experiences and to interpret these experiences differently (Hirschmann and Munter, 2000; Orbach, 2002).

Over time women realise that they are not saturated with dislike of their bodies. There are times when they feel good about themselves and how they look and times when they are not self-conscious about their bodies. When they begin to notice the contradictory and shifting feelings they have about their bodies, women do not as readily assume that when they feel negatively about their body this is 'seeing their body as it really is'. They come to understand that those feelings will shift and change over time. When a client who has recently stopped bingeing and purging tells me that she feels driven to eat and purge when she feels 'like a blimp', she also knows that she does not always see or experience herself this way and that this feeling passes.

These changes do not occur overnight, but women report feeling such relief during the times when they feel 'okay' about their bodies, or are conscious of not hating their bodies, that this serves as a catalyst for them to continue to explore what else they are experiencing. This also allows them to question their previously rigidly held beliefs about their body as only flawed and unacceptable.

Similarly, the meanings women give to food and their relationship with food begin to change. Clare had previously described food as the 'the only thing I look forward to in my day'. Food provided her with comfort, served as a treat, and was imbued with the power to make her feel better when she was stressed or lonely. For many years Clare had followed a rigid diet for a week or two then began overeating and usually binged on and off for the next month before commencing a new diet. Clare's experiences of deprivation when dieting reinforced her belief that food was her friend.

Clare made a decision to stop dieting and to try to resist eating according to whether she judged a food as 'good' or 'bad'. Instead of adhering to some external authority, like the diet sheet or calorie counter, Clare began to approach her eating in a very different way. Without trying to change what she ate, she began to notice whether she was hungry when she ate, whether she felt satisfied after eating and how she had been feeling prior to eating. These questions shifted the meaning of her eating experiences from 'Should I or shouldn't I eat this?' and 'Will this make me fat?' to 'Am I hungry?', 'What do I feel like eating?' and 'Do I feel satisfied?'

Clare noticed that she often binged in the evenings after work when she was at home alone. She realised that, contrary to her previous beliefs about herself, she did not, in fact, eat 'all the time'. There were times when Clare was not overeating and able to leave food on her plate if she was full. This began to shift Clare's understanding of herself from someone who was completely out of control around food to someone who turned to food when confronted with difficult feelings, such as loneliness. Clare developed a compassionate understanding of her difficulties with food, as the meanings she gave to her eating shifted. She recognised that she over-ate not because she was out of control but in an attempt to gain control when she felt overwhelmed by painful feelings. Over time Clare was increasingly able to 'put food back in its right place'. She ate when she was hungry and stopped most often when she was full. Food and eating took on new meanings and resulted in Clare feeling she was 'not the madwoman I'd thought I was'. Clare experienced a freedom from the self-surveillance that had characterised her daily life. Her interest in exploring why she ate when she wasn't hungry led her to learn how to bear her feelings of loneliness without eating in response to them. She learnt to develop alternative strategies for dealing with these feelings.

Differences within and between women

On the view that there is no universally shared experience and understanding of the world and no universal patterns of behaviour, it would be erroneous to suggest that coming through difficulties with food and body could ever be a 'one-size-fits-all' approach. The clinical work is characterised by the difference and diversity within and between women. Attending to 'who sees and how they see' is essential in understanding how individual women make sense of their painful experiences of eating and embodiment. Of course there are similar themes in women's experiences, but there is also enormous variation in the different ways women comprehend and give meaning to their experience. Discourses of race, ethnicity, gender, class, religion and poverty give rise to different meanings and understandings of food and the body (see Thompson, 1994; Waipara-Panapa, 1995). The experience of hunger and the meanings given to food will be different for a woman who was enrolled at Weight Watchers when she was 10 than for a woman who grew up in poverty and went to bed hungry as a child.

Expanded understandings of food, fat and embodiment

Changes in meanings of food and eating, and in how and why we eat, do not mean women will not sometimes feel 'fat' or desire a thinner, more culturally acceptable body. But there is a significant contrast in the meanings of these desires from how women understood them previously. Many women believe that the 'ideal' body is achievable and if not achievable they should at least aim to approximate a thin body size. Women who have been exposed to alternative discourses that privilege cultural explanations for their difficulties, instead of blaming individual women, are more likely to have an understanding of the political and gendered nature of their desire to be thin, although many would not describe their experience in those words.

For many women the overarching desire to be thin wanes as they realize that being 'thin' is not the panacea they once thought it was (Orbach, 1978). When the meanings of being thin are explored, 'thin' is often seen as less important than it was previously and certainly viewed as a more complex and problematic desire. Many women develop a critical awareness of advertising, particularly advertising by the diet industry. Women begin to question and challenge taken-for-granted or common-sense assumptions, that is, we all want to be thin and this is the most important and worthwhile goal for a woman. For many women, being 'thin' becomes less important than it has been previously when they understand how a thinner body had become symbolic of their desires. For one woman her fantasies of being thin might have promised a pain-free existence, for another being thin might have held the promise that her family would take her seriously, and yet another woman might see thinness as promising independence and self-respect. As women come to see that a thin body cannot deliver in this way, they are often able to recognize and pursue their desires more directly.

Some women who have used food to deal with painful feelings learn to be less fearful of what they feel and better able to understand, accept and bear their feelings. This can result in women feeling more confident in their ability to take care of themselves directly, instead of using food to do this. These expanded understandings of food, fat and embodiment can lead to different, more positive experiences for women, for example eating and feeling satisfied, and not feeling frightened of their appetites. Alternative understandings have effects on the body, 'giving it new meanings, hence new feelings, new possibilities for experience and above all, greater acceptance of the fact of one's body' (Garrett, 1998: 181–2). Women's goals tend to shift from a focus on losing weight to a new purpose of wanting to eat in tune with their hunger, wanting to understand why they binged on Friday evening or wanting to make it through a whole week without bingeing and purging.

From individual pathology to a socially constructed world

Women who have experienced difficulties with food and dislike of their bodies have been subject to discursive practices that are punitive and blame individual women for their distress. A discourse of weight-loss blames women for a lack of will-power and the inability to exercise self-control around food, the success of which is measured by women's diminishing size. Failure to lose weight is met with derision. Some women who attended a Weight Watcher's meeting after gaining weight reported that those who had gained weight rather than losing it stood in front of the class, while other – successful – dieters 'oinked' at them like pigs. Ngaire, a woman in her mid-30s, had been referred by her doctor to a dietician because she was 'obese'. As requested, Ngaire took along a food record detailing what she had eaten during the previous week. The dietician took a red pen and 'marked' Ngaire's food record, circling the 'mistakes' she had made with her eating, an experience Ngaire described as 'humiliating'. These practices blame the women who are experiencing distress about their bodies and their eating.

It is no surprise, then, that women blame themselves for their ongoing troubles with food and the difficulties they experience with their bodies. They often believe they are flawed in some way and not good enough or strong enough to stop bingeing or purging, and despair of ever being able to eat like 'normal' people. Many women comment on media images of thin women and the pressure they feel to emulate the 'ideal body', but they believe their own difficulties with food and embodiment occur more or less in a vacuum. A strong individualism operates that locates the cause of their difficulties within their own 'personalities'.

As we have seen, the discourse of body image problems pathologises individual women by blaming them for the distress they feel about the size and shape of their bodies. When a clinician works from a position that there are good reasons why so many women struggle with feeding themselves and feeling comfortable in their bodies, this signals something different to women. They are likely to feel less blamed and ashamed. It introduces the possibility that their eating, often experienced as 'crazy' and 'out of control', might make sense. For example, Sophie was referred to me by her doctor, who had diagnosed her as 'obese'. Initially Sophie would itemise all the food she had eaten during the week, food she judged as 'bad', in the confessional tone of a failed dieter. She seemed to expect a negative or punitive response from me. When I would say, for example, 'I am not surprised that this has been a difficult week for you around food', this communicated the possibility for Sophie to see her own experiences differently. My interest was not in what she ate, but why she might have felt the need to eat when she wasn't hungry and to eat so much that she felt ill afterwards. Working from a position where the purpose is to understand each woman's experience, and the multiple and contradictory meanings that food and body size hold for her, communicates a shift in intention – away from judging or blaming – and signals hope that there is another way for women to make sense of and resolve their difficulties with food.

Women often express disappointment in themselves if they get 'caught up' in wanting to attain what they say they know are impossible standards of physical perfection for women. Many women believe they should be able to resist being negatively affected by cultural representations of women/women's bodies. It is often a relief to women when I question whether this is not an impossible task. I suggest to women that there is 'no outside' of society, that society is like a pot of soup and we are bubbling away in it all the time. Our desires – to be thin, to be accepted, desired, envied – all the ways in which we wish to represent ourselves – are inseparable from cultural representations. To call into question taken-for-granted assumptions about the separateness of the 'individual' and 'society' confounds the familiar, dominant understandings women hold and alerts them to alternative (non-blaming) ways of understanding their own experiences.

Women frequently report being depressed and stuck because they are desperate to lose weight or stop bingeing and purging and then find themselves overeating or vomiting. They feel ashamed of their behaviour because they 'know better' and view their eating patterns as self-destructive. They want to stop using food in these ways, yet have often been unable to do so. Understanding these contradictory intentions and desires is problematic if we insist on a view of the individual as a unitary, rational being. If we understand subjectivity as shifting and contradictory, it becomes possible to explore women's conflicting desires. This can make it possible for women to understand and experience their contradictory impulses without judging themselves as 'mad' or 'bad'.

How women come to think about themselves and 'reality' can only be 'made up' from the cultural beliefs and meanings available to them at any historical moment. The relationship a woman has to her body in Western culture is still, arguably, dominated by the belief that a woman's best attribute is a body that is attractive and acceptable. By looking at our bodies as 'attributes', we become separate or cut-off from our bodies, viewing them as objects that can be manipulated. When we begin to diet, overeat and/or purge, these eating practices contribute to a view and experience of the body as a malleable object, that can be moulded at will (Orbach, 1999; Thompson, 1994). Our perceived failure to achieve the 'right' body weight results in continued disciplinary practices to shape our body and control our – unruly – appetites. Most women I work with are harshly self-critical, either because of their perceived failure to maintain rigid dietary regimes and lose weight, or because they view their eating as self-destructive but feel unable to stop bingeing/purging.

Discourse is a site of production and a site of struggle over the multiplicity of meanings of the body, subjectivity and experience. Marginalised discourses, such as a feminist social constructionist view that locates women's difficulties with eating and embodiment in a clear social and political context, are not readily available or accessible to most women. A feminist social constructionist approach in individual therapy, self-help groups or psycho-educational groups can provide women with access to marginalised discourses which generate alternative, and more useful, possibilities for making sense of their experiences. It is important to acknowledge that many women do make positive changes in their eating and their relationship to their bodies without therapy. Some women do access alternative – positive, feminist – discourses through friends, through books and through their own experiences. For others, spiritual beliefs and practices such as Buddhism and meditation or yoga have given rise to a different – embodied – experience. These practices also place an emphasis on the cultivation of 'inner' bodily awareness, and the development of a compassionate understanding and experiencing of difficult or overwhelming feelings. Changes in bodily experience give rise to knowledge and can enable women to question the meanings they previously gave to their bodies and to begin to change their eating practices.

Approaching our clinical work from a view that women's anxiety about their bodies is a product of social power relations, rather than individual pathology, can enable women to make shifts in the meanings they give to food, eating and their bodies. These shifts in meaning can give rise to different, more positive and pleasurable experiences of food, eating and embodiment.

Note

1. When speaking of women in this chapter, these are women referred to by the authors noted above, as well as women the author has worked with.

REFERENCES

Ackard, D. and Petersen, C. (2001) 'Association between puberty and disordered eating, body image and other psychological variables'. *International Journal of Eating Disorders* 29 (2): 187–194.

Albers, S. (2003) *Eating Mindfully: How to End Mindless Eating and Enjoy a Balanced Relationship with Food*. Oakland, CA: New Harbinger Publications.

Altabe, M. and Thompson, J. K. (1996) 'Body image: a cognitive self-schema construct'. *Cognitive Therapy and Research* 20: 171–183.

Althusser, L. (1971) *Lenin and Philosophy and Other Essays*. London: New Left Books.

American Psychiatric Association (1980) *Diagnostic and Statistical Manual of Mental Disorders*, 3rd edn. Washington, DC: American Psychiatric Association.

American Psychiatric Association (1994) *Diagnostic and Statistical Manual of Mental Disorders*, 4th edn. Washington, DC: American Psychiatric Association.

Barnes, B. and Law, J. (1976) 'Whatever should be done with indexical expressions?'. *Theory and Society* 3: 223–237.

Barthes, R. (1973) *The Fashion System*. New York: Hill & Wang.

Bartky, S. (1988) 'Foucault, feminity and the modernization of patriarchal power'. In I. Diamond and L. Quinby (eds), *Feminism and Foucault, Reflections on Resistance*. Boston, MA: Northeastern University Press.

Beck, A. T. and Freeman, A. M. (1990) *Cognitive Therapy of Personality Disorders*. New York: Guilford.

Berger, J. (1972) *Ways of Seeing*. London: Viking.

Berscheid, E., Walster, E. and Bohrnstedt, G. (1973) 'The happy American body: a survey report'. *Psychology Today* 11: 119–131.

Billig, M. (1987) *Arguing and Thinking: A Rhetorical Approach to Social Psychology*. Cambridge: Cambridge University Press.

Billig, M. (1991) *Ideology and Opinions*. London: Sage.

Billig, M., Condor, S., Edwards, D., Gane, M., Middleton, D. and Radley, A. (1988) *Ideological Dilemmas*. London: Sage.

Blood, S. (1994) 'What other women look like naked: reading a popular women's magazine'. *SITES* Spring: 64–80.

Blood, S. (1996) 'The dieting dilemma: factors influencing women's decision to give up dieting. *Women and Therapy* 18: 109–118.

Bordo, S. (1993a) 'Feminism, Foucault, and the politics of the body'. In C. Ramazanoglu (ed.), *Up Against Foucault: Explorations of Some Tensions Between Foucault and Feminism*. London: Routledge.

Bordo, S. (1993b) *Unbearable Weight: Feminism, Western Culture and the Body*. London: University of California Press.

Boskind-White, M. (2000) *Bulimia/Anorexia: the Binge/Purge Cycle and Self-starvation*, 3rd edn. New York: W. W. Norton.

Bruch, H. (1962) 'Perceptual and conceptual disturbances in anorexia nervosa'. *Psychosomatic Medicine* 14: 187–194.

Bruner, J. (1990) *Acts of Meaning*. Cambridge, MA: Harvard University Press.

Bullerwell-Ravar, J. (1996) 'How important is body image for normal weight bulimics? Implications for research and treatment'. In B. Dolan and I. Gitzinger (eds), *Gender Issues and Eating Disorders*. London: Atlantic Highlands.

Burman, E. and Parker, I. (eds) (1993) *Discourse Analytic Research: Repertoires and Readings of Texts in Action*. London: Routledge.

Butler, J. P. (1990) *Gender Trouble: Feminism and the Subversion of Identity*. New York: Routledge.

Butters, J. W. and Cash, T. F. (1987) 'Cognitive-behavioral treatment of women's body-image dissatisfaction'. *Journal of Consulting and Clinical Psychology* 55: 889–897.

Cash, T. (2002a) 'Beyond traits: assessing body image state'. In T. Cash and T. Pruzinsky (eds), *Body Image, A Handbook of Theory, Research and Clinical Practice*. New York: Guilford.

Cash, T. (2002b) 'Cognitive-behavioural perspectives on body image'. In T. Cash and T. Pruzinsky (eds), *Body Image: A Handbook of Theory, Research and Clinical Practice*. New York: Guilford.

Cash, T. F. and Brown, T. A. (1987) 'Body image in anorexia nervosa and bulimia nervosa'. *Behavior Modification* 11: 487–521.

Cash, T. F. and Fleming, E.C. (2002) 'The impact of body image experiences: development of the Body Image Quality of Life Inventory'. *International Journal of Eating Disorders* 31: 455–460.

Cash, T. F., Fleming, E. C., Alindogan, J., Steadman, L. and Whitehead, A. (2002) 'Beyond body image as a trait: the development and validation of the Body Image States Scale'. *Eating Disorders: The Journal of Treatment and Prevention* 10 (2): 103–113.

Cash, T. F. and Henry, P. E. (1995) 'Women's body images: the results of a national survey in the USA'. *Sex Roles* 33: 19–28.

Cash, T. F. and Labarge, A. S. (1996) 'Development of the appearance schemas inventory: a new cognitive body-image assessment'. *Cognitive Therapy and Research* 20: 37–50.

Cash, T. F., Melnyk, S. E. and Hrabosky, J. I. (2004) 'The assessment of body image investment: an extensive revision of the Appearance Schemas Inventory'. *International Journal of Eating Disorders* 35 (3): 305–316.

Cash, T. F. and Pruzinsky, T. (eds) (1990) *Body Images: Development, Deviance, and Change*, New York: Guilford.

Cash, T. F. and Pruzinsky, T. (eds) (2002) *Body Image: A Handbook of Theory, Research and Cinical Practice*. New York: Guilford.

Cash, T. F., Winstead, B. A. and Janda, L. H. (1986) 'Body image survey report: the great American shape-up'. *Psychology Today* 20: 30–37.

Chernin , K. (1983) *Womansize: The Tyranny of Slenderness*. London: Women's Press.

Chernin, K. (1985) *The Hungry Self: Women, Eating and Identity*. New York: Harper & Row.

Cleo (February, 1993) 'The new meaning of thin'.

Cleo (September, 1997) 'Ten women bare all. Rear views: when did you last see your bottom?'

Cleo (January, 1998) 'Topless and bottomless: women talk about their lives – love me, love my body'.

Cooper, P. J., Taylor, M. J., Cooper, Z. and Fairburn, C. G. (1987) 'The development and validation of the Body Shape Questionnaire'. *International Journal of Eating Disorders* 6: 485–494.

Cosmopolitan (September, 1997) 'Body obsessions'.

Cosmopolitan (January, 1998) 'Men rate their girlfriends' bodies'.

Cosmopolitan (February, 1998) 'Not tonight honey . . . I've got cellulite': how your body image affects your sex life'.

Cosmopolitan (January, 2004) 'Reality-read special 7 Body Battles PLUS body-image IQ quiz': 112–120.

Crisp, A. H. and Kalucy, R. S. (1974) 'Aspects of perceptual disorder in anorexia nervosa'. *British Journal of Medical Psychology* 47: 349–361.

Cusumano, D. L. and Thompson J. K. (2001) 'Media influence on body image in 8–11 year-old boys and girls: a preliminary report on the Multidimensional Media Influence Scale'. *International Journal of Eating Disorders* 29 (1): 37–44.

Dana, M. (1987) 'Compulsive eating: an information sheet for self-help therapy groups'. Unpublished worksheet. London: Women's Therapy Centre.

Dana, M. and Lawrence, M. (1988) *Women's Secret Disorder: A New Understanding of Bulimia*. London: Grafton.

Danziger, K. (1990) *Constructing the Subject: Historical Origins of Psychological Research*. Cambridge: Cambridge University Press.

Diamond, H. and Diamond, M. (1985) *Fit for Life*. New York: Warner.

Dreyfus, H. and Rabinow, P. (1982) *Michel Foucault: Beyond Structuralism and Hermeneutics*. Hemel Hempstead: Harvester Wheatsheaf.

Edwards, D. and Potter, J. (1992) *Discursive Psychology*. London: Sage.

Fallon, A. E. and Rozin P. (1985) 'Sex differences in perceptions of desirable body shape'. *Journal of Abnormal Psychology* 94: 102–105.

Farrell, C., Shafron, R. and Fairburn, C. G. (2003) 'Body-size estimation: testing a new mirror-based assessment method'. *International Journal of Eating Disorders* 34 (1): 162–171.

Feingold, A. and Mazzella, R. (1998) 'Gender differences in body image are increasing'. *Psychological Science*, 9: 190–195.

Fisher, S. (1986) *Development and Structure of the Body Image*, Vol. 1. Hillsdale, NJ: Lawrence Erlbaum Associates, Inc.

Fisher, S. and Cleveland, S. E. (1958) *Body Image and Personality*. New York: Van Nostrand.

Fiske, J. (1987) *Television Culture*. New York: Methuen.

Foucault, M. (1972) *The Archaeology of Knowledge and the Discourse on Language*, New York: Pantheon.

Foucault, M. (1977) *Discipline and Punish: The Birth of the Prison*. New York: Random House.

Foucault, M. (1980) In C. Gordon (ed.), *Power/Knowledge: Selected Interviews and Other Writings (1972–1977)*. Harvester Wheatsheaf.

Foucault, M. (1982) 'The subject and power'. Afterword to H. Dreyfus and P. Rabinow (eds), *Beyond Structuralism and Hermeneutics*. Chicago, IL: University of Chicago Press.

Foucault, M. (1985) *The Use of Pleasure*. Harmondsworth: Penguin.

Foucault, M. (1988) In L. Kritzman (ed.), *Politics, Philosophy, Culture: Interviews and Other Writings, 1977–1984*. London: Routledge.

Foucault, M. (1990). *The History of Sexuality. Vol. 1: An Introduction*. Harmondsworth: Penguin.

Gardner, R. and Boice, R. (2004) 'A computer program for measuring body size distortion and body satisfaction'. *Psychonomic Society* 36 (1): 89–95.

Garner, D. M., Garfinkel, P. E., Stancer, H. C. and Moldofsky, M. D. (1976) 'Body image disturbance in anorexia nervosa and obesity'. *Psychosomatic Medicine* 28: 327–337.

Garner, D. M. and Kearney-Cooke, A. (1997) 'Body image'. *Psychology Today* 30: 55–60.

Garrett, C. (1998) *Beyond Anorexia: Narrative, Spirituality and Recovery*. Cambridge: Cambridge University Press.

Gavey, N. (1992) 'Technologies and effects of heterosexual coercion'. *Feminism & Psychology* 2: 325–331.

Gergen, K. J. (1985) 'Social constructionist inquiry: context and implications'. In K. J. Gergen and K. E. Davis (eds), *The Social Construction of the Person*. New York: Springer-Verlag.

Gergen, K. J. (1991) *The Saturated Self: Dilemmas of Identity in Contemporary Life*. New York: Basic Books.

Gergen, K. J. (1994) *Realities and Relationships: Soundings in Social Construction*. Cambridge, MA: Harvard University Press.

Gergen, K. J. (1996) Unpublished presentation on social constructionism and psychology. University of Auckland, New Zealand.

Gilbert, G. N. and Mulkay, M. (1984) *Opening Pandora's Box: A Sociological Analysis of Scientists' Discourse*. Cambridge: Cambridge University Press.

Goldstein, L. (ed.) (1991) *The Female Body*. Ann Arbor, MI: University of Michigan Press.

Gough-Yates, A. (2003) *Understanding Women's Magazines: Publishing, Markets and Readership*. London: Routledge.

Grogan, S. (1999) *Body image: Understanding Body Dissatisfaction in Men, Women and Children*. London and New York: Routledge.

Grosz, E. (1987) 'Notes towards a corporeal feminism'. *Australia Feminist Studies* 5: 1–17.

Grosz, E. (ed.) (1991) 'Special Issue: Feminism and the body'. *Hypatia* 6: 1–3.

Grosz, E. (1994) *Volatile Bodies: Toward a Corporeal Feminism*. Bloomington, IN: Indiana University Press.

Haraway, D. (1991) *Simians, Cyborgs, and Women: The Reinvention of Nature*. New York: Routledge.

Heinberg, L. J. and Thompson, J. K. (1995) 'Body image and televised images of thinness and attractiveness: a controlled laboratory investigation'. *Journal of Social and Clinical Psychology* 14: 325–337.

Heinberg, L. J., Thompson, J. K and Stormer, S. (1995) 'Development and validation of the sociocultural attitudes towards appearance questionnaire'. *International Journal of Eating Disorders* 17: 81–89.

Henriques, J., Hollway, W., Urwin, C., Venn, C. and Walkerdine, V. (1984). *Changing the Subject: Psychology, Social Regulation and Subjectivity*, London: Methuen.

Hepworth, J. (1999) *The Social Construction of Anorexia Nervosa*. London: Sage.

Hirschmann, J. and Munter, C. (1988) *Overcoming Overeating*. New York: Ballantine.

Hirschmann, J. and Munter, C. (1995) *When Women Stop Hating Their Bodies*. New York: Ballantine.

Hirschmann, J. and Munter, C. (2000) *Overcoming Overeating*, 2nd edn. London: Random House.

Hollway, W. (1989) *Subjectivity and Method in Psychology: Gender, Meaning and Science*. London: Sage.

Hsu, L. K. (1982) 'Is there a disturbance in body image in anorexia nervosa?'. *Journal of Nervous and Mental Disease* 170: 305–307.

Hsu, L. K. and Sobkiewitz, T. A. (1991) 'Body image disturbance: time to abandon the concept for eating disorders?'. *International Journal of Eating Disorders* 10 (1): 15–30.

Hundleby, J. D. and Bourgouin, N. C. (1993) 'Generality in the errors of estimation of body image'. *International Journal of Eating Disorders* 13: 85–92.

Knapp, C. (2003) *Appetites: Why Women Want*. New York: Counterpoint.

Lakoff, G. (1987) *Women, Fire and Dangerous Things: What Categories Reveal About the Mind*. Chicago, IL: University of Chicago Press.

Lawrence, M. (1984) *The Anorexic Experience*. London: Women's Press.

Lawrence, M. (ed.) (1987) *Fed Up and Hungry: Women, Oppression and Food*. London: Women's Press.

Loates, L. (1992) 'Naked Truths. A special report: what other women look like naked – women talk about their bodies'. *More* October: 43–44.

McCracken, E. (1993) *Decoding Women's Magazines: From Mademoiselle to Ms*. New York: St. Martins Press.

McNay, L. (1992) *Foucault and Feminism*. Cambridge: Polity Press.

Malson, H. (1998) *The Thin Woman: Feminism, Post-structuralism and the Social Psychology of Anorexia Nervosa*. London: Routledge.

Mandler, J. M. (1979) 'Categorical and schematic organization in memory'. In C. R. Puff (ed.), *Memory, Organization and Structure*. New York: Academic Press.

Marie Claire (March, 1997) 'Body image: how do you shape up?'.

Marie Claire (March, 2001) 'Love it, loathe it or just live with it: real women rate their bodies'.

Matus, J. L. (1995) *Unstable Bodies: Victorian Representations of Sexuality and Maternity*. New York: Manchester University Press.

More (April, 1994). 'Mirror, mirror....'

Morris, S. (1992) 'Editor's introduction: what other women look like naked'. *More* October: 3.

New Weekly (September, 1994) 'What's wrong with your body?'

New Weekly (May, 1997) 'Women with real thighs and the men who love them'.

New Woman (January, 1997) 'Are you obsessed with your looks?'

New Woman (April, 1997) 'The bad news about body image'.

N.Z. Woman's Weekly (June, 1995) 'Which of these women likes her body?'

Norris, D. L. (1984) 'The effects of mirror confrontation on self-estimation of body dimensions in anorexia nervosa, bulimia and two control groups'. *Psychological Medicine* 14: 835–842.

'O' (The Oprah Magazine) (October, 2001) 'Special: build a better body image. Feel good naked'.

Orbach, S. (1978) *Fat Is a Feminist Issue*. London: Arrow Books.

Orbach, S. (1982) *Fat Is a Feminist Issue II*. London: Hamlyn Paperbacks.

Orbach, S. (1986) *Hunger-strike*. London: Faber & Faber.

Orbach, S. (1988) *Fat Is a Feminist Issue*, 2nd edn. London: Arrow Books.

Orbach, S. (1999) *Towards Emotional Literacy*. London: Virago.

Orbach, S. (2002) *On Eating: Change Your Eating, Change Your Life*. London: Penguin.

Peeke, P. (2000) *Fight Fat After Forty: How to Stop Being a Stress Eater and Lose Weight Fast*. Bodmin, UK: MPG Books.

Petrie, A., Tripp, M. and Harvey, P. (2002) 'Factorial and construct validity of the Body Parts Satisfaction Scale – Revised: an examination of minority and non-minority women'. *Psychology of Women Quarterly* 26 (3): 213–221.

Polivy, J. and Herman, P.C. (1987) 'Diagnosis and treatment of normal eating'. *Journal of Consulting and Clinical Psychology* 55 (5): 635–644.

Potter, J. and Edwards, D. (1992) *Discursive Psychology*. London: Sage.

Potter, J. and Wetherell, M. (1987) *Discourse Analysis and Social Psychology: Beyond Attitudes and Behaviour*. London: Sage.

Potter, J. and Wetherell, M. (1994) 'Some practical issues in analyzing discourse'. In J. Smith, R. Harre, L. van Langenhove and P. Stearns (eds), *Rethinking Psychology*. London: Sage.

Radley, A. (1991) *The Body and Social Psychology*. New York: Springer-Verlag.

Robertson, M. (1992) *Starving in the Silences: An Exploration of Anorexia Nervosa*. Sydney, Australia: Allen & Unwin.

Rose, G. (1993) *Feminism and Geography*, Minneapolis, MN: University of Minnesota Press.

Rose, N. (1990) *Governing the Soul: the Shaping of the Private Self*. London: Routledge.

Rose, N. (1996) *Inventing Ourselves: Psychology, Power and Personhood*. Cambridge: Cambridge University Press.

Rosen, J. C., Srebnik, D., Saltzberg, E. and Wendt, S. (1991) 'Development of a body image avoidance questionnaire'. *Journal of Consulting and Clinical Psychology* 3: 32–37.

Rosen, J. C., Saltzberg, E. and Srebnik, D. (1989) 'Cognitive behavior therapy for negative body image'. *Behavior Therapy* 20: 393–404.

Roth, G. (1983) *Feeding the Hungry Heart*. New York: Penguin.

Roth, G. (1986) *Breaking Free from Compulsive Eating*. London: Grafton Books.

Roth, G. (1989) *Why Weight? A Guide to Ending Compulsive Eating*. New York: Penguin.

Roth, G. (1996) *Appetites: On the Search for True Nourishment*. New York: Dutton.

Ruff, G. A. and Barrios, B. A. (1986) 'Realistic assessment of body image'. *Behavioral Assessment* 8: 237–251.

Sawicki, J. (1991) *Disciplining Foucault: Feminism, Power and the Body*. New York: Routledge.

She&More (February, 1998) 'What I really think about my body: real women strip bare to share their most personal feelings'.

She&More (November, 1998) 'Does size matter? Women talk about body image'.

Schilder, P. (1935) *The Image and Appearance of the Human Body: Studies in the Constructive Energies of the Psyche*. London: Kegan Paul.

Schulman, R. G., Kinder, B. N., Powers, P. S., Prange, M. and Cleghorn, A. (1986) 'The development of a scale to measure cognitive disturbance in bulimia'. *Journal of Personality Assessment* 50: 630–639.

Secord, P. F. and Jourard, S. M. (1953) 'The appraisal of body-cathexis: body-cathexis and the self'. *Journal of Consulting Psychology* 17: 343–347.

Shontz, F. C. (1969) *Perceptual and Cognitive Aspects of Body Experience*. New York: Academic Press.

Showalter, E. (1987) *A Female Malady: Women, Madness and English Culture, 1830–1980*. London: Virago.

Slade, P. (1985) 'A review of body-image studies in anorexia nervosa and bulimia nervosa'. *Journal of Psychiatric Research* 19: 255–265.

Slade, P. (1994) 'What is body image?', *Behaviour, Research and Therapy* 32: 497–502.

Slade, P. and Russell, G. F. M. (1973) 'Awareness of body dimensions in anorexia nervosa: cross-sectional and longitudinal studies'. *Psychological Medicine* 3: 188–199.

Smith, D. E. (1990) *Texts, Facts and Femininity: Exploring the Relations of Ruling*. New York: Routledge.

Spitzack, C. (1990) *Confessing Excess: Women and the Politics of Body Reduction*. New York: State University of New York Press.

Thompson, B. W. (1994) *A Hunger So Wide and So Deep*. Minneapolis, MN: University of Minnesota Press.

Thompson, J. K. (1986) 'Larger than life'. *Psychology Today* 20: 39–44.

Thompson, J. K. (1990) *Body Image Disturbance: Assessment and Treatment*. Elmsford, NY: Pergamon.

Thompson, J. K. and Heinberg, L. (1999) 'The media's influence on body image disturbance and eating disorders: we've reviled them, now can we rehabilitate them?'. *Journal of Social Issues* 55 (2): 339–353.

Thompson, J. K., Heinberg, L. J. and Clarke, A. J. (2001) 'Treatment of body image disturbance in eating disorders'. In J. K. Thompson (ed.), *Body Image, Eating Disorders and Obesity: an Integrative Guide for Assessment and Treatment*. Washington, DC: American Psychological Association.

Thompson, J. K., Penner, L. and Altabe, M. (1990) 'Procedures, problems and progress in the assessment of body images'. In T. Cash and T. Pruzinsky (eds), *Body Images: Development, Deviance, and Change*. New York: Guilford.

Thompson, J. K. and Smolak, L. (eds) (2001) *Body Image, Eating Disorders and Obesity in Youth: Assessment, Prevention and Treatment*. Washington, DC: American Psychological Association.

Traub, A. C. and Orbach, J. (1964) 'Psychophysical studies of body-image: the adjustable body-distorting mirror'. *Archives of General Psychiatry* 11: 53–66.

Ussher, J. (1989) *The Psychology of the Female Body*. London: Routledge.

Ussher, J. (1991) *Women's Madness*. Hemel Hempstead: Harvester Wheatsheaf.

Ussher, J. (ed.) (1997a) *Body Talk: the Material and Discursive Regulation of Sexuality Madness, and Reproduction*. London: Routledge.

Ussher, J. (1997b) *Fantasies of Femininity: Reframing the Boundaries of Sex*. Harmondsworth: Penguin.

Waipara-Panapa, A. (1995) 'Body and soul: a sociocultural analysis of body image in Aotearoa/New Zealand'. Unpublished thesis, University of Auckland.

Weedon, C. (1987) *Feminist Practice and Poststructuralist Theory*. Oxford: Basil Blackwell.

Wetherell, M. (1996) 'Analysing discourse; interpretive repertoires and ideological dilemmas'. In J. Maybin and N. Mercer (eds), *Using English: From Conversation to Canon*. London: Routledge.

Wetherell, M. (1998) 'Positioning and interpretive repertoires: conversation analysis and structuralism in dialogue'. *Discourse and Society* 9: 431–456.

Wetherell, M. and Maybin, J. (1995) 'The distributed self'. In R. Stevens (ed.), *Understanding the Self.* London: Sage.

Wetherell, M. and Potter, J. (1992) *Mapping the Language of Racism: Discourse and the Legitimation of Exploitation.* London: Harvester Wheatsheaf.

Wetherell, M. and White, S. (1992) 'Fear of fat: young women talk about eating, dieting and body image'. Unpublished manuscript.

Winship, J. (1987) *Inside Women's Magazines.* London: Pandora.

Wolf, N. (1990) *The Beauty Myth.* London: Chatto & Windus.

INDEX